# The Ironmen

# The Ironmen

## The 1939 Hawkeyes

Scott M. Fisher

Copyright © 2003 by Scott M. Fisher.

Cover: University of Iowa Football Squad following Spring Practice 1939 (courtesy: University of Iowa Archives)

Library of Congress Number:    2003091987

ISBN :      Hardcover         1-4010-9045-1
            Softcover         1-4010-9044-3

All rights reserved. No part of this book may be reproduced or transmitted in any form or by any means, electronic or mechanical, including photocopying, recording, or by any information storage and retrieval system, without permission in writing from the copyright owner.

This book was printed in the United States of America.

**To order additional copies of this book, contact:**
Xlibris Corporation
1-888-795-4274
www.Xlibris.com
Orders@Xlibris.com
17590

# Contents

Preface: 2nd Edition .................................................. 9
Preface: Original Edition ......................................... 13
Acknowledgments: Introduction ........................... 17
Chapter 1: The Early Thirties ................................. 23
Chapter 2: Forging the Iron ..................................... 34
Chapter 3: Preseason ............................................... 50
Chapter 4: South Dakota: First Blood ..................... 53
Chapter 5: Indiana: First Conference Game ........... 60
Chapter 6: Michigan: First Road Trip ..................... 71
Chapter 7: Wisconsin: Rebound .............................. 81
Chapter 8: Purdue: On the Road—Again ............... 91
Chapter 9: Notre Dame: Home at Last ................... 98
Chapter 10: Minnesota: Invasion from the North ... 107
Chapter 11: Northwestern: Finale ......................... 120
Chapter 12: Aftermath ........................................... 130
Chapter 13: Nile Kinick: The Quiet Leader ........... 136
Chapter 14: Letters ................................................. 140
Chapter 15: An Interview with Nile Kinnick ........ 160
Bibliography—Print Sources ................................. 167

This book is dedicated to the memory of Eugene L. Fisher—University of Iowa Athlete, member of the Iowa Football Coaches Hall of Fame, gifted teacher, respected civic leader, and my grandfather—without whose help and encouragement this could never have been completed.

. Dedication (Second Edition)

This edition is dedicated to the memory of Eugene L. "Bud" Fisher – Iowa State Teachers College Athlete, member of the University of Northern Iowa Athletics Hall of Fame, gifted teacher, respected civic leader, and my dad – without whose wisdom and guidance I could never have become a successful teacher and writer. And to his two athletic grand daughters: Melissa and Elizabeth Kidder.

# PREFACE

## 2ND EDITION

It's been almost twenty years since I started the initial research for *The Ironmen*. The project, originally part of a master's thesis, was inspired by stories I had heard as a kid in Davenport and Cedar Falls, listening to my grandfather and his brothers, all Iowa athletes, talk about college football's "old days" when they played "in the stadium across the river" at Iowa—long before face masks, Spandex, or "TV" time outs. My dad and his brother, also college athletes and Iowa high school football coaches, took it to the next generation, of Nile Kinnick and the Ironmen, describing college football "before the war" when they were kids.

Through those family connections, I was able to locate some of the members of that '39 Hawkeye team, and those men, in turn, "handed me off" to other squad members and others who had been part of that era. I'll always be especially grateful to Max Hawkins, my very first personal interview for a writing project. He sat patiently with me in his living room on Melrose Avenue in Iowa City as I fumbled through a list of questions and had forgotten to check the batteries on my tape recorder. It was just the first of well over a hundred interviews I conducted, both in person and by telephone, for this book. There have been hundreds more since then for dozens of other writing projects, but I'll always remember that first one with Max in the shadow of Kinnick Stadium.

The joy of corresponding with so many of that "greatest generation" has not faded with time. However, it is sad and ironic that several of the men who were so generous with their time and memories passed away just before the first edition was published: Max Hawkins, Jens Norgaard, Chuck Tollefson, Wally Bergstrom and Nile Kinnnick's father, Nile, Sr., with whom I had many wonderful visits.

Two other memories stand out from when I put the first book together. The first was the several days I spent at the University's Special Collections department at the library at the invitation of Mr. Bob McCown. The boxes containing the diaries, letters, recordings and photographs donated by Nile Kinnick's father is a truly inspiring collection. In those boxes are glimpses of a young man who was much more than a star athlete. Here is a complex person who spent every waking moment filling his young life with experiences that he could learn from, and use later to make the world a better place. It is interesting that the questions he has about society and humanity are the same ones young men and women in college have today. That collection is also a reminder of how very often the "best and the brightest" are sacrificed in wars. One of his teammates probably described him best: "He was just . . . Kinnick, an indescribable human being." That says it all.

On a lighter note, the other wonderful memory I have is the weekend of the 50th anniversary Ironmen reunion in Iowa City. It started on Friday afternoon when I shared a table at Iowa Book and Supply with Al Couppee and Erwin Prasse for a book signing session that brought in all kinds of people: other '39 Hawkeye teammates, retired members of the faculty, young fans getting books and autographs for their parents who lived far away, and even a few older visitors who remembered the "Fisher Boys" of yesteryear. Later that evening, my dad and I enjoyed the Ironmen reunion banquet, seated at a table surrounded by members of that '39 team, along with their families. It was fun to listen to the banter between the backs and linemen, something that hasn't changed in football, and the recollections of the more humorous side of that season. It was a weekend I'll never forget and I truly appreciated the compliments about the book from those who had actually lived the story.

This edition of *The Ironmen* is about 90% the same as the first. There have been no omissions, except for some photos which were difficult to acquire this time. There are a few new photos and some additional information in each chapter, supplied by many of the team members after they read the first book.

There are two additional chapters as well, one where I included excerpts from letters I received during and after the research for the first edition. Included are comments from some of the Ironmen themselves, some of their opponents that season, and some "special fans" like Nile Kinnick, Sr. and Loren Hickerson who was a personal friend of young Nile. The other new chapter is a transcript of a radio interview that Nile did with Arch Ward on the eve of the 1940 College All-Star football game in Chicago against the Green Bay Packers, for which Nile received the highest number of votes by the fans. The actual tape, along with several others, is located at the University of Iowa Library Special Collections area, to whom I'm very grateful, as always.

The acknowledgements for this edition remain virtually the same as for the first. Sadly, very few of those mentioned in the 1989 book are left now to read this "new and improved" version. I do wish to thank everyone who sent such complimentary letters after reading the first book, whether it was purchased or borrowed from their local library. I hope you enjoy this edition even more.

Scott M. Fisher—2003

# PREFACE

## Original Edition

It is safe to say there will never be another football team like the 1939 Hawkeyes. For one thing, college football has changed immensely in the last fifty years. There are no more "sixty minute" men. Equipment and playing fields have changed both the style and pace of the game. The concept of the student-athlete has evolved greatly since the 1930s. Also, athletes today are bigger, stronger and faster than ever before. All of this has obviously changed the game. It is for fans and sportswriters to argue whether it is for better or worse.

I never saw the '39 Hawkeyes play, except in old films. But my dad and grandfather did, along with a host of other Iowa football fans, who told their kids about the fantastic come-from-behind finishes and rousing upsets by the little band of Hawkeyes. The stories survive to this day—a few of them exaggerated, but not by much.

Nile Kinnick's name is still spoken throughout the Midwest with pride, adulation, and sadness. His achievements on the field may be surpassed, but his combination of dedication, inspiration, and talent will forever remain an unattainable goal.

His awards and honors are well-deserved. But he would be the first to point out (and did so) that it was a team effort and any credit for the surprising success of that 1939 season must go to the group as a whole.

Just as Hawkeye stars of today are compared to, but never equal Nile Kinnick, the great Iowa teams will always be compared to, but never equal: **THE IRONMEN**

# ACKNOWLEDGMENTS

This project could not have been attempted, let alone completed, without the help of many people, to whom I owe my thanks:

To those members of the 1939 Iowa Football Team, who were kind enough to respond, either by letter, telephone, or in person, to my many questions. Thanks to Max Hawkins, Carl Vergamini, George "Red" Frye, Wally Bergstrom, Robert Herman, Bill Diehl, Mr. and Mrs. Chuck Tollefson, Jens Norgaard, and a very special thank you to Al Couppee.

To the "Old Timers" who set the stage for the Ironmen and had to endure the seasons of hardship and frustration of the early thirties: Russ Fisher, Raymond Fisher, and Ozzie Simmons.

To the "Opponents" of the Ironmen, who, win or lose, were quick to praise the spirit of that Hawkeye team they faced: Forest Evashevski, George "Sonny" Franck, Emil "Moose" Uremovich, Harold Van Every, and Robert Flora.

To Nile Kinnick, Sr. and Loren Hickerson, who kindly sent me books and clippings, as well as their priceless thoughts about Nile.

To Robert McCown, of the University of Iowa Library, who allowed me the pleasure and honor of reading Nile Kinnick's diaries, letters, and papers to discover what a unique individual he truly was.

To the helpful people of the Alumni Associations and Archives of the University of South Dakota, Indiana University, the University of Michigan, the University of Wisconsin, Purdue

University, Notre Dame University, the University of Minnesota, Northwestern University, and George Wine and Don Roberts at the University of Iowa.

To Gene Raffensperger of the *Des Moines Register*, whose suggestions and encouragement have been so valuable.

To Robert Bogue, Jack and Dakota Cline, Judy Sharkey, Nancy M. Fisher, Anne and Bruce Kidder, and Leon Ostrander III for putting up with football stories during years of research.

To my dad, Dr. Eugene L. Fisher, Jr., whose stories of the Ironmen and Nile Kinnick told to me years ago during his Iowa coaching days, planted the seed for this project.

Scott M. Fisher
Warren, Michigan 1989

# INTRODUCTION

## AUTUMN, 1939.

Those of us in Iowa were hungry for some good news. True, the Great Depression had savaged the Farm Belt, but by 1939 it was beginning to loosen. War was underway in Europe and its undertow threatened the United States.

As usual Hawkeye football fans looked to Iowa City for some encouragement. Frankly, there had been little to cheer about recently. The 1937 Iowa team had a 1-7 record. The 1938 Hawkeyes were 1-6-1. Four of those losses were shutouts.

So now it was 1939. Iowa had a new head coach, Dr. Eddie Anderson, who came to Iowa in the spring after compiling a fine record at Holy Cross. Anderson, an All-American during his college career at Notre Dame, was a native of Oskaloosa and graduate of Mason City High School. He promised no miracles. He demanded hard work. His no-nonsense approach to the game and tough conditioning tactics left him with just a thin brigade as fall practice started.

Their leader was a 5 foot, 9 inch, 175 pound, pre-law student named Nile Kinnick. He was a back who, ran, passed, punted, and drop-kicked extra points.

And Kinnick played defense, too.

Indeed, as the 1939 season wore on, many of the Iowa starters played both offense and defense. It was a team quality that was to inspire a nickname that has endured 50 years, and will be remembered in Iowa as long as football is played. Ironmen.

Iowa opened the 1939 season with a 41-0 rout of South Dakota. Nice, but no cigar. South Dakota wasn't a Big 10 team. The next week a Big 10 team came to town, Indiana. Hawkeye fans hoped for the best, but seats for the game in Iowa Stadium went begging. The sports editor of the *Waterloo Courier* thought so little of the Iowa-Indiana game he decided to cover Iowa State Teachers College that Saturday.

Iowa beat Indiana, 32-29. The issue was decided on a late pass from Kinnick to Erwin Prasse. The Hawkeyes lost the next week to Michigan, then reeled off consecutive wins over Wisconsin, Purdue, Notre Dame, and Minnesota. The season ended with a 7-7 stalemate at Northwestern. Iowa was 6-1-1.

After that the individual players and coaches began to collect awards. Kinnick won the Heisman Trophy, the only player to date from the University of Iowa to win this most prestigious football award.

Kinnick was also named All-America and was voted the Outstanding Male Athlete of the Year. In addition, Mike Enich and Erwin Prasse were named All-America. Kinnick, Prasse, Buzz Dean, and Dick Evans were selected to the *Chicago Tribune* All Star Team. Anderson was named Coach of the Year.

Now, Scott Fisher has pulled this drama of football and the Ironmen and a state's love and respect for the sport and the team into a marvelously exciting book.

Scott lives in Michigan, but has sturdy Iowa roots having grown up in Davenport. His grandfather, Gene Fisher, was one of Iowa's premier high school football coaches at West Branch and Cedar Falls. Gene's brothers, Darrell, Raymond and Russ, all were football letter winners at Iowa, with Russ captaining the 1934 Hawkeyes. Scott's father, Gene (Bud) Fisher was an outstanding player in high school at Cedar Falls and later a superb college player and Little All-American at Iowa State Teachers College. Later, Bud coached in Davenport and today is a school administrator in Michigan.

For those of us alive during the 1939 season, Scott Fisher has rekindled warm and wonderful memories. For you who were not there to share the drama and excitement, his accounting will put you there.

Gene Raffensperger, *The Des Moines Register*
          Des Moines, Iowa—1989

## 1939 TEAM MEMBERS

| Name | Position | Home Town |
| --- | --- | --- |
| BJ "Bruno" Andruska | Center #14 | Chicago, IL |
| Gerald Ankeny | Quarterback #11 | Dixon, IL |
| Wallace Bergstrom | Tackle #44 | Winfield, IA |
| Russell Busk | Halfback #60 | Clinton, IA |
| Ambrose "Ted" Callahan | Guard/Tackle | Pocahontas, IA |
| John Clemens | Guard | Cedar Rapids, IA |
| Carl Conrad | Guard/Tackle #23 | Fonda, IA |
| Albert Couppee | Quarterback #30 | Council Bluffs, IA |
| Floyd "Buzz" Dean | Halfback #12 | Atlantic, IA |
| William Diehl | Center #29 | Cedar Rapids, IA |
| Jack Edling | Center #16 | Moorhead, MN |
| Lawrence Ely | Guard/Tackle | Des Moines, IA |
| Mike Enich | Tackle #33 | Boone, IA |
| Richard "Whitey" Evans | End #35 | Chicago, IL |
| George Falk | Halfback | Des Moines, IA |
| George "Red" Frye | Center #19 | Albia, IA |
| William Gallagher | Quarterback #25 | Oskaloosa, IA |
| Burdell Gilleard | Halfback #50 | New London, IA |
| William Green | Fullback #43 | Newton, IA |
| Max Hawkins | Guard #64 | Philadelphia, MS |
| Robert Herman | Guard/Tackle | Landsburg, KS |
| Warren Junge | Guard/Tackle | Davenport, IA |
| Robert Kelley | Guard/Tackle | Sioux City, IA |
| Nile Kinnick | Halfback #24 | Omaha, NE |
| Robert Leighton | Guard/Tackle | Spencer, IA |
| Henry Luebcke | Guard #88 | Chicago, IL |
| John Maher | End | Davenport, IA |
| John "Jack" McKinnon | Halfback | Perry, IA |
| Edwin McLain | Halfback #20 | Wauwatosa, WI |
| Matthew Miletich | Guard/Tackle #36 | Chariton, IA |
| Joseph Moore | End #65 | Ida Grove, IA |
| James "Ray" Murphy | Fullback #69 | Great Neck, NY |
| Jens Norgaard | End #21 | Iowa City, IA |
| James Robert Otto | Tackle #31 | Fort Dodge, IA |

| | | |
|---|---|---|
| Roger Pettit | Halfback | Logan, IA |
| Ken Pettit | End #39 | Logan, IA |
| Erwin Prasse | End #37 | Chicago, IL |
| Fred Smith | End #55 | Cedar Rapids, IA |
| Herman "Ham" Snider | Guard #52 | Iowa City, IA |
| Carl Sullivan | Halfback | Chariton, IA |
| Stephen Swisher | Guard | Des Moines, IA |
| Phil Strom | Guard/Tackle | Fort Dodge, IA |
| Charles "Chuck" Tollefson | Guard #27 | Elk Point, SD |
| Carl Vergamini | Guard/Tackle | Council Bluffs, IA |
| Henry Vollenweider | Fullback #49 | Dubuque, IA |
| James Walker | Tackle #63 | South Bend, IN |

# CHAPTER 1

## THE EARLY THIRTIES

Like the nation's economy, the University of Iowa's football program had enjoyed a period of rich growth during the decade of the twenties. By 1929, the new stadium was completed—a tribute to the vision and hard work by University officials and boosters. However, like the stock market, this would prove to be the peak of success for the Hawkeyes for some time to come.

As 1930 rolled around, Iowa was facing unprecedented problems in its athletic department in general and its football program in particular. For various reasons, a "changing of the guard" was taking place.

Gone was the dynamic, though controversial, Howard Jones, whose Hawkeye teams had dominated the early twenties with a record 20 consecutive victories and back-to-back undefeated conference championships. Jones had resigned in 1924, after repeated friction between himself and B.J. Lambert, Chairman of the Board in Control of Athletics. The Iowa head coach took his talents elsewhere—eventually to the University of Southern California, where his Trojan teams would win five Rose Bowls.

Gone, also, was the hard-driving talent of such men as Gordon Locke, Duke Slater, Aubrey Devine, and Willis Glassgow, just a few of the outstanding Iowa grid players of the era.

Burton A. Ingwersen had been hired from Illinois to take over at the helm. Because of his youth (age 26) and his Illini alma mater, many of the Iowa alums were vocal about their displeasure at his hiring. Although his teams from 1924 to 1931 compiled a winning record of 33-29-4, the pressure became too great on all concerned, and Ingwersen resigned after the 1931 season, during which the Hawks won only one game.

The team had moved into its new stadium in 1929, but even the new facility could do nothing to ease the tension. Before the blow felt from Wall Street in October of that year, came a different blow in May from the Commissioner of the Big Ten (or Western) Conference, Major John L. Griffith. Iowa was suspended indefinitely from the conference.

There were many allegations regarding the cause of the suspension. Among these were charges of improper use of scholarships and tuition refunds to aid athletes. This, along with the discovery of an alumni slush fund used for paying local businessmen for the "employment" of athletes, made up the main part of the conference's case against Iowa. There were also the lesser charges that Iowa teams had used non-registered students and professional athletes on varsity teams. There was also an investigation of possible kickbacks paid to athletes through the sale of yearbooks.

The question of proper recruiting of athletes was not a new one at Iowa (nor at most of the other large schools in the conference). As early as 1924, the University had been warned by the Commissioner about "overenthusiastic alumni recruiting athletes and the use of a fund to do that." To help solve the problem, a rule was passed by the conference in 1927 to prohibit excessive participation of alumni in recruiting athletes.

Coach Ingwersen was not the only one undergoing a lot of criticism. There were several movements by alumni groups to force his resignation, along with that of Dr. Belting, the Athletic Director.

Belting, interestingly enough, resigned just before the announcement was made about the suspension, and there were some questions about his part in the wrongdoings. However,

Commissioner Griffith told members of the alumni organization that they (the alumni) "... were more to blame for the situation at the university ..." than those in charge of athletics. He made it clear, also, that the major charge, while not specific, was that the Iowa Athletic Department was not being controlled by the University.

The suspension was to officially begin January 1, 1930—after the 1929 football season. Iowa was not the only member of the conference under suspicion. In fact, one member of the Commissioner's office felt that the University of Chicago was the only school with a "clean slate." But Iowa was the only school penalized—perhaps because the problem was the most serious and obvious there, or perhaps as an example for the other schools to "shape up."

The negative publicity was devastating to the Hawkeye athletic program. All but three major letter winners were declared ineligible for competition. Football, although the hardest hit in the long run, was not the only sport to lose athletes. Members of the basketball, baseball, track, and swimming teams were also declared ineligible—fourteen athletes in all.

The action occurred just in time for the scheduling meetings for the conference. Iowa's indefinite suspension made the other schools shy away from agreeing to include the Hawks in any schedule for the future seasons. Purdue was the only school that tentatively included Iowa in the 1930 schedule. Some members went so far as to declare "... we will never play Iowa." The athletic department was forced to put together a makeshift schedule. Games for 1930 were set up with Oklahoma A & M, Centenary of Shreveport (Louisiana), and the University of Detroit.

Meanwhile, the Iowa administration was desperately trying to put the house in order. The suggestions made by the Big Ten Commission were followed. That, along with a published study by the Carnegie Foundation for the Advancement of Teaching (stating that only Illinois and Chicago had no charges or irregularities under investigation), persuaded the Commission to reconsider. The suspension was rescinded on February 1, 1930—one month after it had been officially imposed.

But the damage had already been done. The clouds of suspicion which had rolled over Iowa City like a thunderstorm took the form of a foggy drizzle. Prospective athletes decided on other schools and the budget for athletics dipped sharply. Even with a weak schedule, the Hawkeyes could manage only a 4-4 season. For 1931, Indiana, Minnesota, and Northwestern joined Purdue on the schedule, but Ingwersen resigned after the dismal 1-6-1 season.

Oscar Martin "Ossie" Solem of Drake University was hired to turn the situation around. Having had eleven successful seasons at nearby Drake, he was familiar with the University of Iowa's plight, but he was not prepared for what he inherited. Once in Iowa City, he discovered that certain promises had not been kept regarding tuition payments and loans for his players. Because of delays and "misunderstandings," he had less than two weeks to put together a team for the 1932 opener against Bradley Tech, which the Hawkeyes won 31-7. It would be their only win of the season.

With suspicions again being circulated about indiscretions in the athletic department (not regarding football), part-time jobs for athletes were practically nonexistent. Solem would not be put off. He worked hard to recruit athletes from within the state and bargained with campus officials and local citizens to find jobs for his players. People were still gun-shy about the recent suspension and reluctant to help. But some progress was made. Things were improving for 1933.

Raymond Fisher, an end on that squad, recalled that small loans were available and that he had a job watering the greens on the University golf course at night. Russ Fisher, Ray's brother and future captain of the 1934 Hawkeyes, worked as a bus boy at the local Elks Club. He said, "In those days, Solem had a training table from August to November, so during that time, those were our meals. The rest of the winter we lived on hamburgers. You could buy five for a quarter. Some of the guys lived in the field house. All they had to do in return was have a fire drill once a month."

The 1933 team, led by quarterback Joe Laws, Captain Tom Moore and All American Francis "Zud" Schammel, started strong—winning three in a row, including two conference upsets of Northwestern and Wisconsin. Dick Crayne, of Fairfield, Iowa, showed his talent by rushing for 181 yards in the Northwestern game, averaging 6.2 yards per carry. Bert McGrane, noted writer for the Des Moines Register, officiated as head linesman in that game. Iowa was dubbed the "surprise team of 1933" and wound up the season with a respectable record of five wins and three losses.

At the Chicago scheduling meetings, Solem had to fight for his share of five conference games—few conference members, for various reasons, wanted to play the Hawkeyes. When Solem made it clear that he wasn't going to leave the meeting " . . . until I get my five games . . ." some modifications were made to accommodate him. Because of poor crowds in Iowa City (which lowered a visiting team's "cut" at the gate), however, many of the games, even non-conference, would have to be played on the road.

Solem's contract was extended to 1938 and he had been named Athletic Director. Most people, including the coach himself, predicted 1934 as a "promising" season. Dick Crayne, returning at fullback, would handle most of the punting chores. With Joe Laws gone, Russ Fisher, the new Hawkeye captain, was moved to the quarterback spot.

There was also a promising newcomer to the team. Ozzie Simmons, who had been an all-state high school quarterback in his native Texas, had made the 1500 mile journey north by freight train to play for Iowa. Fifty years later, the former star explained, "Recruiting was low then at Iowa because of the suspension. One of the alumni wrote to me in Texas and I knew that Iowa offered good opportunities to black athletes. So I wrote to Iowa, but got no reply."

So, Ozzie, his brother, Don (who lettered as an end and

fullback for Iowa), and a few friends decided to make the trip anyway and give it a try. All coaches dream of having "walk-ons" like Ozzie Simmons. He simply showed up in Coach Solem's office one day, asking to play for Iowa. About Solem, Ozzie remarked, "He probably could have been tougher [on the players] but he was the finest gentleman I've ever been around."

The 1934 season opened with strong victories over South Dakota and Northwestern. The third game was on the road against a tough Nebraska team at Lincoln. In those days, teams made the long trips by train. Russ Fisher remembered that night: "We got on the train and went to sleep, expecting to wake up in Lincoln, but the next morning, we were still in the Iowa station because of a wreck down the line."

They finally did make it to Nebraska, but lost a heartbreaker 14-13. It was their first of three losses in a row—one to Iowa State who would not play the Hawkeyes again for many years. Injuries took their toll. Simmons and Fisher were hurt and the team would not really be whole again until the game against Indiana.

The Hoosiers were celebrating homecoming, but the weather was uncooperative. The rain was torrential. It was so bad that at one point the game had to be stopped to allow the rain to let up so the players, not to mention the fans, could see. Although the contest ended in a scoreless tie, an event occurred that is still talked about when Iowa football is discussed. Russ Fisher describes the action: "Dick Crayne stood deep in our own end zone to punt. There was a stiff wind at his back, but the punt was still a great one. The ball went ninety yards past the line of scrimmage before it hit the ground. It skidded the last thirty or forty feet in the mud out of bounds on the Indiana five-yard line." Overall, the ball had traveled 102 yards!

Even with such amazing feats, the Hawkeyes finished the 1934 season no better than 2-5-1. Injuries and a tough schedule of road trips hurt the team. Dick Crayne and Ozzie Simmons would be returning to continue their attempt to build a winner. Simmons had been dubbed the "Ebony Eel" and his running style compared to that of Red Grange.

By 1935, Solem had received permission to supervise the janitorial services in the fieldhouse and some of the other campus facilities. This gave him the opportunity to hire athletes for the work. At last—a regular, dependable source of employment for athletes.

Ozzie Simmons was in exceptional form that year. The All-American led the Hawkeyes to an improved 4-2-2 season with an outstanding performance including 192 rushing yards in the 19-0 upset of Illinois. The 1935 game against Minnesota marked the beginning of the battle over "Floyd of Rosedale," a live pig that year wagered by the states' governors. The tradition continues today, although "Floyd" is now a metal trophy—easier to house and clean. The Gophers won the game 13-6. Ozzie Simmons remembered Minnesota as being " . . . big and tough and one of the great teams of all time. I played safety and got knocked out three times on tackles and had sense enough to sit down the last time."

In 1936, a new group of freshmen arrived on the scene. Solem referred to Erwin Prasse, Dick Evans, and a small halfback named Nile Kinnick as his "best crop yet." The varsity, despite some individual outstanding performances, could not put it together. Winning none of their conference games, they closed out the season with a 3-4-1 record—also closing out Ossie Solem's career at Iowa. After the 1936 season, he resigned and became head coach at Syracuse. He had turned down several other good coaching offers in previous years, saying he wanted to make a go of it at Iowa. It became clear that, although a remarkable recovery from the suspension years had been made—largely due to Solem's efforts—a change was necessary.

Irl Tubbs was hired from the University of Miami for the 1937 season. He announced that he was glad to be back in the upper midwest, having coached nine years at Wisconsin State Teachers College. He also stated that no contract was necessary as he would do his best and let the chips fall where they may.

Although the 1937 season was disastrous in the won-loss columns—1-7, with six straight defeats, there were some bright spots. In several games, the Hawkeyes had statistically been better than the opponent, only failing in the scoring department. Sophomore Nile Kinnick established himself as a quality triple-threat back. His punting and running exhibition, especially in the Wisconsin game, was remarkable.

His passing, especially to another sophomore, Erwin Prasse, was outstanding. Kinnick's teammates gave him the nickname "Hard Rubber" because of his strength and endurance. He finished the season named to the All-Midwest first team and NEA All-America second team. Along with junior end Bob Lannon, Kinnick was named to the first team of the AP Big Ten. The future was bright for this rising star whose dedication on the field was second only to his poise and intellect in the classroom.

*Nile C. Kinnick, jr. (courtesy: University of Iowa Archives)*

*Erwin Prasse, end and team captain
(courtesy: University of Iowa Archives)*

By 1938, a talented group of players had been assembled. There were glimmers of hope, but injuries, as in the promising 1934 season, kept the team from realizing its full potential.

Nile Kinnick injured his ankle early in the year and was only a shadow of the 1937 star. Firm in his Christian Science beliefs, he would accept no treatment for the injury—not even ankle wraps or X-rays. Though the pain must have been excruciating, he maintained his competitive nature and remained a threat as a punter. Al Couppee, a future Iowa quarterback and a freshman that season, recalled about Kinnick's injury, "It's probable the ankle was fractured. You could see the pain in his face when he punted."

The Hawkeyes dropped their first two games of the 1938 season to set a record of eight consecutive defeats. In the second game (a 31-13 loss to Wisconsin) a young Hawkeye named Mike Enich put on quite a defensive exhibition. His hard tackles and ability to shed blockers gave the Badgers a tough time. On one play, he tackled both the ball carrier and his blocker.

Iowa's losing streak was finally broken in the third game, against the University of Chicago (soon to leave the Big Ten). The 27-14 victory marked the first Iowa win over another Big Ten team since 1935. It would be their only victory of the season.

The Purdue game resulted in a scoreless tie with the Hawkeyes playing above their capability. It was actually seen as a victory. But the 1-6-1 season ended with Iowa scoring only three points in the last five games and only forty-six all year.

There had been some outstanding performers, however. Kinnick finished fourth in the nation in punting with a 41.12-yard average. Erwin Prasse was named to the All Big Ten All-Star first team with Kinnick an honorable mention. Nile summed up his thoughts about his frustrating season in a letter to his parents: "I have had the courage of my convictions in those things which needed such a decision. It has not been a lot of fun nor has it been a displeasure, but certainly this fall has not been without its fruits—unseen though they may be."

About the game in general, he wrote, "I am far from being soured on football; I enjoy it and look forward to next season, but I deplore the shape it is taking and regret that the athletes are being exploited in the interest of a misguided public opinion."

Coach Tubbs requested that the University permit the football players to live together in one house with a training table. University officials flatly refused and pointed out that the athletic department had lost over $10,000 in 1938 and they were not about to spend any more. Tubbs resigned.

So, for the third time in eight years, Iowa was looking for a new head coach. Everyone had opinions about a successor and this time virtually all of the parties were listened to: get a Notre Dame man; get a man from Iowa; get a man with a proven record.

They hired a man who fit the bill in all categories. His name was Dr. Edward Anderson.

# CHAPTER 2

## FORGING THE IRON

Iowa alumni and boosters had never forgiven the University for allowing the chance of hiring Knute Rockne to slip through its fingers years before—although the chance had been slim at best. Since that time, there had been pressure on the administration to hire a coach from Notre Dame. There was also pressure from a large group to hire an Iowan, who could relate to the people and problems of the Corn State.

When Dr. Edward N. Anderson signed a three-year contract (for $10,000 per year) in Boston's Plaza Hotel, both groups had what they wanted. In fact, members from both groups had traveled to Boston, some under assumed names, to sign the Holy Cross coach before that team's season ended.

Anderson was born in Oskaloosa, Iowa, on November 11, 1900. After graduation from Mason City High School, the quiet, sandy haired end headed for Notre Dame. There he played for the legendary Knute Rockne and with the immortal George Gipp. Of Anderson, Rockne later said that he never saw the young man knocked off his feet. The Irish were beating everybody and had rolled up a winning streak of twenty-two consecutive games (including back-to-back 9-0 seasons during Anderson's sophomore and junior years). The bubble finally burst, ironically, at the hands of Iowa, in 1921, when Anderson was the Notre Dame Captain and All-American.

Fresh with his Notre Dame-style of football, Anderson took a job as head football coach at Columbia College (Loras) in Dubuque, Iowa. His three-year record there included sixteen wins, six losses, one tie, and one undefeated season. During his first year, he was considered as a possible assistant coach at Iowa, but Howard Jones, the Hawkeye head coach, rejected the idea.

From Dubuque, Anderson went to the Chicago area to attend Rush Medical College. That alone would seem to be enough to keep anyone busy. But Anderson also coached football at DePaul University and acted as player/coach of the Chicago Cardinals professional football team.

Upon his graduation as a specialist in urology, "Dr. Eddie" as he liked to be called, was hired by Holy Cross College, in Worcester, Massachusetts, to revive their football program. His success was amazing and almost immediate. From 1933 to 1938, his teams accumulated a startling record of 47-7-2, with undefeated seasons in 1935 and 1937.

*Dr. Eddie Anderson (courtesy: University of Iowa Archives)*

When Irl Tubbs resigned at Iowa, Anderson's name came up almost at once as a possible successor. Wanting to establish a head coach as quickly as possible, the University "bent the rules" a little and worked out the Boston deal. Always enjoying a challenge, especially at a Big Ten school and close to his home town, Anderson agreed to the terms. The coach said he would report to Iowa City immediately following the conclusion of the 1938 season.

On November 29, 1938, Anderson, along with his staff of ex-Notre Damers, signed the papers in Iowa City, making everything official.

Jim Harris, who had been the line coach at Holy Cross, would continue in the same capacity at Iowa. Harris, always quick with a witty remark, had the distinction of being the last substitute ever sent into a football game by Knute Rockne. Joe Sheeketski would be the backfield coach. (He would leave, however, before spring practices, to become the head coach at Holy Cross.) Bill Osmanski, Andersen's outstanding fullback at Holy Cross, agreed to help out with the spring drills before reporting to the Chicago Bears.

Dr. Eddie began the task of reviewing his personnel. If he was to begin to build a winning program, he had to know who he could count on and who had the leadership qualities. He wanted to meet as many of the returning lettermen and promising freshmen as possible. He also met with the University officials and athletic directors to be sure there was no lack of communication regarding tuition payments and jobs for athletes. During all of this, he somehow found time to serve as a urologist at the University of Iowa Hospital.

Anderson had inherited a very diverse group of hopeful young men. The handful of returning lettermen had experienced defeat and humiliation during their careers. But there was a number of youngsters who were still excited enough to keep the spirit alive.

It was truly a cross-section of men. Some of the players were somewhat older, having spent a few depression-era years in the service or working at various jobs before coming to Iowa. Some were well-to-do—others dirt poor. Some came from large families—others orphaned or with just one parent. Some hailed from crowded cities—others just off the farm. Anderson knew he had to pull the group together if they were to be successful.

The captain of the Hawkeyes was Erwin T. Prasse, of Chicago. The 6'2", 190-pound left end was All-Big Ten in 1938 and had been voted Most Valuable Player by his teammates. The Shurz High School graduate was a three-letter man for Iowa. In addition to football, Prasse excelled as a guard on the Hawkeye basketball team and played second base on the baseball diamond.

Dick "Whitey" Evans, another Windy City product, played at the other end. Evans, described as quiet and very sensitive, was a graduate of DePaul Academy in Chicago. At 6'3" and 190 pounds, he was also a member of the basketball squad. Behind Prasse and Evans at the end positions were Fred Smith and Jens Norgaard. Smith, one of the two black players on the team was 6'2", 200 pounds and was described by teammates as "one tough blocker." Norgaard, a junior, loved to tangle in scrimmages. The son of a Danish sea captain, Jens and his family had moved to the United States in 1926, following the loss of most of their savings because of speculation on the German mark. Jens' mother, an American, had a sister in Iowa, and the family settled in Iowa City where she supported her two sons and daughter as a beautician. Jens was All-State in football during his high school days.

There was an abundance of talent at the tackle position. Mike Enich, a 6'2", 212-pound native of Boone, Iowa, had been an All-State fullback during his prep years and had played in the backfield on the 1938 Hawkeye squad. Tait Cummins, noted Iowa sportswriter, described Enich as "pure gold" and "the kind of fellow any father would like his son to be."

Jim Walker, from South Bend, Indiana, was the other black player on the team. Known for his hard-driving blocking ability, he also excelled on defense.

Wally Bergstrom was one of the older members of the team. The 6'2", 200-pound tackle from Winfield, Iowa, had attended the University earlier and left school to work on a coffee boat in South America. After a couple of years, he returned to Iowa City. Although quiet and unassuming, he was always ready to go when needed.

Three other Iowa natives were available as tackles: Matthew Miletich of Chariton, James Robert Otto of Fort Dodge, and Carl Conrad of Fonda.

There was no lack of talent at the guard position. At 6'4", and almost 300 pounds (nobody really knew for sure), Henry "Hank" Luebcke was the biggest and strongest man on the team. But Anderson, disturbed by Luebcke's excessive weight, told the Chicago native that in order to play, he would have to get down to around 265 by fall. Luebcke went on a rigid diet and exercise program and later made weight. Unfortunately, during the spring workouts, nobody knew for sure if he would make it. Thus, he got less of a chance to show his talent and surprising speed.

Herman "Ham" Snider had been an all-stater for Iowa City High School in 1936. The quick-witted guard was only 5'9", 190 pounds and had barrel shoulders and bowed legs, but had tremendous desire and a wise-crack for any situation.

Ken Pettit was a former All-State back from Logan, Iowa. Anderson moved the 6'1", 185-pounder from end, where he had played in 1938, to guard. Ken was one of the most sensitive and sincere players on the team and was the younger brother of Roger, another older player. Roger had been a star in the early thirties at Thomas Jefferson High School in Council Bluffs. A terrific punter, he decided to attend Iowa with Ken after working at various jobs.

Charles "Chuck" Tollefson was another older member. He was from the dairy farm country of Elk Point, South Dakota. Like Wally Bergstrom, Tollefson had attended Iowa earlier in the decade, left for a few years in the working world, and had returned to school—a hard thing to do, especially in those times. Next to Hank Luebcke, Chuck was the strongest man on the squad.

Max Hawkins, also at guard, hailed from Philadelphia, Mississippi. He had played in the backfield in high school. After a half-year at Mississippi State, Max left school and lived with an uncle in Texas before joining the navy in 1933. He distinguished himself playing service football and was named "All-Fleet." It was also good experience in that his teams occasionally scrimmaged against professional football teams like the Los Angeles Bulldogs. Upon his discharge in 1937, Hawkins had arranged to attend Temple University, but happened to meet the Iowa coaches and was persuaded to lend his experience and leadership to the Hawkeyes. From his home in Iowa City fifty years later, he acknowledged his admiration for Anderson, describing him as a "smart coach who could handle men." About his teammates, he stated, "We were a team of over-achievers."

The center position proved to be the most punishing. Bill Diehl, a sophomore from Cedar Rapids, was a transfer student from Temple University. One of the brightest members of the team, he quickly picked up on Andersen's complicated offense.

Bruno Andruska, a 6-foot, 184-pound junior, and one of the few returning lettermen, was a graduate of Leo High School in Chicago. He could excel, despite painful injuries.

George "Red" Frye, of Albia, Iowa, was another who immediately took to Anderson and his philosophy of "positive thinking." Fifty years later, he said affectionately of Anderson, "He's the only physician I've known who believed running was the cure for everything from a sprained ankle to a missed signal."

Rounding out the available centers was Jack Edling, another welcome out-of-stater from Moorhead, Minnesota.

At fullback, James R. "Ray" Murphy, Jr. was upholding a family tradition. His father had played fullback and captained the 1911 Hawkeyes. Despite a problem with poor eyesight, Ray, Jr. proved himself to be a tough blocker—even against his own teammates. Many were temporarily put out of action in practice after receiving a crushing block from the lean 6'2", 184-pounder. Like his good friend, Ham Snider, Murphy always had a clever remark handy.

Bill Green, another fullback, was said to have had the greatest athletic ability of anyone on the squad. He was certainly one of the fastest. The 6'1", 185-pound sophomore had been a record-breaking track star in high school in Newton, Iowa. He was described by Tait Cummins, who traveled with the team, as "just an overgrown kid who laughs and jokes his way through practice."

Another fleet-footed fullback was Henry Vollenweider. He had been a championship hurdler in high school at Dubuque.

While not a primary ball-carrier, the quarterback of the pre-war era, as in today's game, was usually the field general. Intelligence and good leadership qualities were important. Aptly suited for the job was Al Couppee who was called "the personification of a field general and born-to-be a leader." The 6', 190-pound sophomore was an all-state back out of Thomas Jefferson High School in Council Bluffs where he had also starred in basketball, track, baseball, and boxing.

Gerald Ankeny, from Dixon, Illinois, was another one who loved to block and mix it up with anyone. Although something of a country boy, he was quick to learn Anderson's complicated offense and was an able leader. Bill Gallagher was another hopeful at the quarterback position. He was from Dr. Eddie's home town of Oskaloosa, Iowa.

The "glory men"—the halfbacks—were few in number but long on talent and desire. Ed McLain played on the right side. The 6-foot, 188-pound senior was a letterman from the two previous seasons and hailed from Wauwautosa, Wisconsin, where he had attended Lake Forest Academy. Floyd "Buzz" Dean was another Iowan, from Atlantic. He had almost chosen to attend Coe College, but picked Iowa in the end. Russell Busk, of Clinton, Iowa, was one of the smallest members of the team. His surprising speed earned him the nickname "Rabbit."

And, of course, at left halfback was Nile Kinnick. Nile Clarke Kinnick had grown up in Adel, Iowa, and had played American Legion baseball with Bob Feller. His father, Nile Sr., was a prominent banker in the area and quite an athlete in his own right. The Kinnick brothers, Nile and Ben (a year apart in age) and the youngest, George, were raised in an environment of hard work, strong discipline, and family togetherness.

Nile showed his athletic skills at an early age when he and brother Ben led the Adel Junior High School football team to an undefeated season. In 1933, The Adel High School Tigers, with Nile as star performer, recorded the first-ever undefeated football season. That same year, Nile led the basketball team to the district championship finals, as a junior forward.

In 1934, Nile's father moved the family to Omaha, Nebraska, because of great economic crisis that was hitting the banking business, not to mention the rest of the country. The Kinnicks watched as more than one of their family farms were lost. Nile spent his senior year at Benson High School in Omaha.

The older Kinnick brothers developed a successful passing combination for the "Benson Bunnies." It was Nile completing passes to Ben and both of them scoring touchdowns that sparked the offensive charges. And it was Nile, once again in the forward position, that led Benson to a third-place finish in the state basketball tournament. He finished out his one-year career at Benson by leading them to a city baseball championship.

All of the headlines and awards could not sway Nile from his true modesty and respect for the team effort. He was always quick to give credit to teammates and to worthy opponents. When it was time for college, there was no doubt that Nile would go to Iowa. While not exceptionally big (5'9", 175 pounds) or fast, his drive and desire to be the best, along with an excellent mind, gave him the tools to come as close to perfection as anyone can— both in physical achievements and personal character. Just before the beginning of the 1939 spring workouts, Nile wrote to his parents, "For three years, nay for fifteen years, I have been preparing for this last year of football. I anticipate becoming the roughest, toughest, all around back yet to hit this conference." He also wrote, "I am looking forward to showing Anderson what a real football player looks like—so hold your hats."

With any team, especially great winning teams, there is a multitude of people who contribute just as much as the regular players. In a way, they contribute more because much of their contribution is unnoticed by fans and sportswriters. These important individuals have the courage to endure the pain and drudgery of practices and meetings, often without any chance of playing regularly—sometimes not at all. Yet, without them, no team can be great. Their importance, though often unrecognized in print, is not unnoticed by grateful coaches, teammates, and knowledgeable fans.

Some, like Carl Vergamini, of Superior, Wisconsin, suffered injuries during the season that required them to leave the team. Others, like Robert Herman, of Landsburg, Kansas, could not recover from spring-time injuries and subsequent operations sufficiently to be with the team in the fall.

Many, like Burdell "Oops" Gilleard, Johnny Maher, and Phil Strom, were gifted athletes, unfortunately playing behind other gifted athletes. John "Jack" McKinnon of Perry, Iowa and Joseph Moore gave each practice session their best effort to show the starters the right "look" in preparation for upcoming games. Competitors like Warren Junge, John Clemens, and Stephen Swisher took the lumps and kept going. Carl Sullivan, Ambrose Callaghan, Robert Leighton, William Berryhill, and Larry Paul withstood the blazing heat, bone-chilling cold, and seemingly endless practices to be a part of a new beginning. Robert Kelley, Lawrence Ely, and George Falk knew the pain of the nagging hurts, but also knew the importance of their roles.

There were also the support people like Willard Hayne, the team doctor, who was just out of University of Iowa Medical School, assisted by Doyle Alsup, in his first year as team trainer. Also on the staff were: Elwyn Shayne, the equipment manager and his assistant "Old Sarge" Lemmons. Without them, the team would not even have been able to suit up. In addition, there were dozens of volunteer and student assistants, maintenance personnel, and fans who, although they never received formal recognition, played major roles in the formation of the 1939 Hawkeyes.

Following a rousing welcome by boosters and students on the steps of Old Capitol, Eddie Anderson and his staff wasted no time in meeting with as many of the local supporters as possible. Some, like Hi Jennings, provided meeting space and acted as liaison to other local people in order to introduce the new coaches to the community. Speaking engagements were arranged for Anderson, the assistant coaches, and some of the players.

Anderson met individually with his players on various evenings on the second floor of the downtown Jefferson Hotel. Some of the younger athletes, like Al Couppee, had toyed with the idea of leaving Iowa in the spring in search of more successful programs.

Couppee recalled his meeting with Anderson, some of the new staff, and the lettermen one night at the hotel: "He [Anderson] grabbed me by the hand and looked me right in the eye and slapped me on top of the shoulder and turned around to Joe Sheeketski, and with that typical Anderson sort of bravado, he said, 'Joe, look at this. He's got plenty of blockin' space up there hasn't he? Plenty of blockin' space!' Then he slapped me on the shoulders again. And, of course, I'm eighteen years old and thought that's the greatest thing that ever happened to me. That kind of turned my whole thinking around right there—just the force of his personality and that little incident, it carried over to all the rest of the guys. It was leadership personified."

It was Anderson's trait to grasp and squeeze a man's hand hard when he first met him to see "what kind of meat the guy had." Only two players, Hank Luebcke and Chuck Tollefson, could match his vise-like grip. Dr. Eddie made it clear that strength and skill on the field were not the only requirements he expected. He said, "We want student athletes at Iowa. They make the best players over the long run, anyhow. I want players who'll fight to live, not who fight 'till they drop." Although, later on, more than one would do just that.

The initial test for everyone would come in spring practice and Anderson's calendar showed the first day of spring as February 1, 1939—at least as far as football was concerned. He opened the practices up to all comers and a surprising number of about 85 hopefuls showed up. He told them, "The team in the best condition will win," and he proceeded to demonstrate his point. Many of the group fell by the wayside before long.

Joe Sheeketski was named as Anderson's successor at Holy Cross and had departed for the East. The new backfield coach, Frank Carideo, had been Notre Dame's quarterback during Knute Rockne's national championship teams of 1929 and 1930. Rockne had called Carideo " . . . another coach on the field." In fact, Carideo had been one of Rockne's pall bearers following the coach's death in a plane crash.

In his senior year, Carideo, who had learned his punting skills under LeRoy Mills, was the number one kicker in the nation. He also held a college career record of 1006 yards in kick-off returns. Before joining the Iowa staff, he had coached at Mississippi State.

Bill Hofer, another former Notre Dame quarterback (a teammate of Joe Sheeketski), was hired to help with the spring drills. He would act as coach of the freshmen the following fall.

Carl Vergamini, who was trying to get back in shape after knee surgery, remembered the spring workouts as "intense and well-run." Al Couppee recalled the practices as "brutal—lots of running, running, running." The new head coach worked hard to teach the Hawkeyes the new offensive system. The style was basically Rockne's Notre Dame offense with some innovations by Anderson.

Most plays originated from a "Tight-T" formation from which the play was called—huddles were seldom used. The quarterback usually called the play when the team lined up. Unlike today, the quarterback, in this system, seldom handled the ball and hardly ever threw a pass. He was primarily a blocking back and receiver.

Some of the plays, such as quick-openers—designed to catch the defense off guard—could be run from the T-Formation. However, most of the time, the backs shifted into the Notre Dame "Box" formation which had the left halfback and fullback side by side in the backfield, the right halfback moving out to a wing position, and the quarterback moving up close to the line between the guard and tackle on the same side as the wing back. The ball was usually snapped directly to the "tailback," or left half, who could hand off, pass, run it himself, or kick, depending on the situation.

There were also some plays designed to be run from short or long punt formations. All formations had variations, such as designating an interior lineman as an eligible pass receiver.

When the play was called on the line of scrimmage, the quarterback yelled three single-digit numbers, followed by three double digit numbers, such as: 8-7-2; 43-25-32. In the first set of numbers, the last digit (2) told the team what pattern or version of a certain play was going to be run. In the second set of numbers, the first digit (4) would denote the direction the play would go. An even number meant the play would be to the right. An odd number meant left. Also in the second set of numbers, the second digit of the first number (3) and the first digit of the second number (2) told the number of the play (#32—the "2" version). The rest of the numbers meant nothing. From this information, every player knew what to do when the ball was snapped.

After calling the play, either the quarterback or tailback yelled the "count": Hike! One! Two! Three! Four! On "Hike!" the backs began their shift from the T-Formation to the Box-Formation (or any other formation they had planned.) The shift was complete by the "Three!" count so everyone was motionless for the required one second. The ball was usually snapped on "Four!" However, sometimes a long count was used and the snap was delayed to five or six to perhaps draw the defense offside.

With all of the innovations and variations possible from each play, the offense was not an easy one to learn. There was no room for players of poor intelligence. Anderson drilled the system into the young men's minds until they were dreaming about it.

The defense was nothing fancy. As with most teams of that era, a 6-2-2-1 (that is, six down linemen, two linebackers, two halfbacks, and a safety man) or a 5-3-2-1, were the standard defenses. Much of the pass coverage was man-to-man, although occasional zone coverage was used in some situations.

Players played "both ways" meaning that a man would play a certain position when his team had the ball and stayed in the game at a defensive position when the other team had the ball. If a substitution was made during the game, the new player could not talk to his teammates for one play. This limited the amount of information that could be sent into the game from the sidelines. If a team used a huddle just after a substitution, an official would enter the huddle to make sure the new player did not pass along any information.

Anderson's practices started at 4 p.m. sharp. Nile Kinnick was the first man on the field—sometimes long before the others—and usually the last man off. Often, he and Frank Carideo worked on Nile's punting and drop-kicking. They practiced by the hour either before or after the normal practice session—sometimes both. Nile's ankle had fully healed and he wrote to his parents proudly that he was not wrapping his ankles, or doing any other preventive measures that might conflict with his Christian Science beliefs. Although some of the other men did not understand his reasoning, they respected his faith and dedication—especially as they watched him punt that "curve ball" into the coffin corner of the field time after time.

Nile wrote to his brother, George: "Frank Carideo, our new backfield coach, was one of the best quarterbacks and the nation's best punter in his day. Already he has started to work with the kickers, and would you believe, the way he recommends to hold the ball, the way to stand, everything is exactly the way I have practiced all my life. My passing is better than ever—I even whip them out time after time with my left hand—and accurately too."

The combination of Kinnick's restored health and Carideo's tutoring brought great results. Anderson, a good judge of character, knew that Kinnick never had to be driven or pressured—he did enough of that to himself. On the practice field, Anderson would call each player by his last name, whether in praise or criticism—except Kinnick. With him, it was always "Nile."

*Assistant Coach Frank Carideo (left) and Nile Kinnick practice punting (courtesy: University of Iowa Archives)*

Red Frye recalled that during practices if a player sustained a minor injury, Anderson would tell him to "run it off." Dr. Eddie, Frye said, was constantly reminding ball carriers, "Never run out of bounds! Get every inch!" and "Run over them, not around them."

By late spring, due to the strain of conditioning, the punishing contact drills, and the complicated offense, about fifty of the original group had been eliminated—most on their own. Others had been sidelined due to injury. A common joke was directed at Ray Murphy who, because of his punishing blocks, was "accused" of causing a number of team injuries. Sometimes there weren't enough healthy players to conduct a decent scrimmage. After a particularly tough practice, as Red Frye remembered, Anderson closed the session with the comment, "We didn't do much today, but will give it hell tomorrow."

Much of the practice time was spent running plays against different defenses. In fall practices, Freshmen were often used on scout teams to give the varsity a good "look" at what they might be up against. Sometimes it was punishing to the ineligible freshmen, but most of them knew it was their chance to show the coaches what kind of talent was available and waiting for next year. Other times, plays were run against dummies to work on timing and small details.

The last part of practice was usually spent running plays up and down the length of the field. The first team lined up on the goal line, followed by the second team and third, if there were enough players. The quarterback called the play and the men ran each one about thirty yards or so until they reached the opposite goal, at which time they would turn around and run plays back. It would not be unusual for them to make ten or more laps of the field.

Al Couppee recalled, " . . . the guys always wanted me to call plays in which somebody other than Kinnick carried the ball. Why? Well, when I called a play with Kinnick carrying the ball, he always sprinted forty or fifty yards and placed the ball on the ground and ran back so as to be in immediate position for the next play to be called. If the other guys didn't keep up with Kinnick, it became readily apparent to the coaches, and they proceeded to chew out some rear ends. Kinnick just didn't know any other way to practice but full speed all the time."

Frank Carideo was especially tough on the men during these drills. The players would looked forward to hearing the city's six o'clock rocket because they knew once they heard it, sometime within the next twenty or thirty minutes practice would be over. On one such evening, Carideo was being particularly hard on the first team and the players were telling Al Couppee (between gasps) to try to slow things down a little. They had hardly stood still for an instant when Carideo's voice came booming through the twilight, "If you can't run that team, Couppee, I'll get somebody who can!" Before the sound of his voice had died away, a voice from the first team came back through the gloom, "O.K., Markov!" It was Buzz Dean, who had recently seen the movie *Beau Geste* and had been impressed by the tortuous Sgt. Markov character. Ever after that evening, the backfield coach was known as Markov Carideo—a title he thoroughly enjoyed.

By June first, it was over. Only about 35 men were left out of the group that had started a few months earlier. Those who had "survived" felt they were ready. Anderson and his staff had given them every reason to believe they could be winners in the fall. The players were impressed with their new coaches and the new system. Hopefully, the feeling would be retained through the summer as the young men went their separate ways.

There were those who were not so confident or hopeful. Bill Osmanski, upon his departure from his temporary coaching position, was quoted as saying, "Among 5000 male students at the University of Iowa, there are only five real football players." The test of the validity of that statement would come in the fall.

# CHAPTER 3

## PRESEASON

The fall of 1939 was a landmark year in college football. Sportswriters were predicting a year with the accent on speed and more use of the forward pass. In 1938, there had been eight football fatalities due to skull fractures. With the use of head protection now mandatory, the outlook was for a safer season as well.

During the winter and spring months there was much discussion about rule changes—especially concerning the use of time-outs. Elmer Layden, Notre Dame's head coach advocated a rule "which would prohibit all time-outs during the last three minutes of the game, except in case of genuine injuries." However, no agreement was reached.

There was heated talk and finger-pointing concerning recruiting. Several northern schools had been severely warned about violations, thus causing college officials to cut back on some scholarships and jobs for athletes. Some of the spokesmen from the Big Ten felt that southern schools were getting away with violations. Some were quoted as saying, "If those Confederates don't stop coming up here with their money bags for ammunition, there's going to be another Civil War." All of this made for great journalistic drama and would make contests between northern and southern teams even more newsworthy.

Sportswriters picked Notre Dame as the powerhouse, although Midwestern coaches seemed to agree on Purdue as the most fearsome. When the various polls came out, as far as the Big Ten was concerned, Michigan, Minnesota, and Northwestern were heavy favorites, followed by Purdue, Wisconsin, Indiana, and Ohio State. Iowa could do no better than "long shot" status.

Of the major "neutral" publications that fall, only the *Saturday Evening Post* offered some upbeat words about the Hawkeyes. Francis Wallace, in his annual "Pigskin Preview," said, "Iowa is on the rebound. Eddie Anderson, new head coach, inherited a good first team. Nile Kinnick, recovered from 1938 injuries, is potentially one of the stars of the year."

*Nile Kinnick warming up his passing arm (he could pass with either hand) (courtesy: University of Iowa Archives)*

When it came to rating the teams and backs, the *Post* picked Tennessee's George "Bad News" Cafego as the potential number one back for the year. Others at the top of the list were: Bob Saggau of Notre Dame; Bruce Smith of Minnesota; Lou Brock of Purdue; and Wisconsin's George Paskvan and Bob Cone.

Bert McGrane asked several of the younger Iowa players what the Hawkeyes' chances were for the upcoming season as they gathered for preseason practice. He was probably surprised to hear the replies of optimism. When he asked Al Couppee to explain why the young quarterback felt that Iowa's future was so bright after such a poor showing the previous year, the cocky sophomore replied, "They didn't have me last year."

Late in September, Anderson called for the team's first major scrimmage. Although it was nothing spectacular, he called it an "encouraging performance." The team was small with only about thirty-five members, but they were eager.

Saturday, September 30th, 1939 would tell the real tale. That was when the Hawkeyes were scheduled to play their opener against the Coyotes of the University of South Dakota.

# CHAPTER 4

## SOUTH DAKOTA: FIRST BLOOD

A skeptical, yet hopeful crowd of 16,000 fans filed into Iowa stadium on Saturday, September 30th, 1939. South Dakota already had a game under its belt, having been beaten by only six points by College of the Pacific, coached by Alonzo Stagg.

For home games, Eddie Anderson had his team stay on Friday nights in a secluded ward at the University Hospital, away from the distractions of pre-game celebrations and other festivities. It allowed the young men to have some time to relax, get a good night sleep, along with knowing exactly where they were. After a pre-game meal, the squad walked down to the stadium and entered at the southeast corner. It was down a short flight of steps to the locker room where they "put on their armor" as Al Couppee liked to say. About 40 minutes before game time, Anderson would walk into the open space in the middle of all the lockers and go over what sort of warm-up drills they would do, then the team moved out of the locker room, down a long flight of stairs and out onto the grass.

Before this particular game, Dr. Eddie got all of the quarterbacks together and told them not to use the whole offense. Knowing there would be scouts from future opponents in the stands, he limited his team to certain basic plays. Fred Smith, Buzz Dean, and Robert Herman were recovering from injuries and their availability was doubtful. Everyone else was in shape and anxious to play.

The starting lineup was Bill Diehl at center; Chuck Tollefson at left guard and Hank Luebcke (he had made weight) at right; Jim Walker at left tackle and Mike Enich at right; Captain Erwin Prasse at left end with Dick Evans on the right side; Al Couppee at quarterback; Nile Kinnick at left halfback and Russ Busk at right; Ray Murphy and Bill Green would alternate at fullback.

***William Diehl, center (courtesy: University of Iowa Archives)***

The 1939 season began with Prasse's kick-off to the Coyotes. The first series of plays for each team were uneventful.

Wernli, of South Dakota, punted to Kinnick who made a good return to the Iowa 40-yard line. Runs by Murphy, Ed McLain, and Kinnick moved the ball to the visitors' 47-yard line. But Kinnick was forced to punt and he got off a beauty that rolled out of bounds on the South Dakota nine.

Wernli punted the ball right back, only to his own 35-yard line. But the Hawkeyes fumbled away their first opportunity with good field position. Fortunately, they were able to hold the Coyotes.

This time, Wernli's punt sailed to the Iowa 25-yard line where it was downed.

On the first play, the "Rabbit"—Russ Busk—scampered around left end for ten yards and a first down. This excited the crowd and made the defenders spread out a little. On the next play, Kinnick took the ball through a hole on the right side made by Luebcke and Enich. He did not stop until he crossed the goal line 65 yards away. His successful drop kick for the extra point made the score: Iowa 7-South Dakota 0.

Prasse's second kick-off of the quarter went to Trompeter who managed a good return to his own 42-yard line. He was injured during the tackle and was replaced by Taplett.

The Coyotes decided to try an aerial attack and Anderson went back to pass under heavy pressure by the Iowa line. The ball was intercepted by Bill Green, who was tackled close to midfield. A twelve-yard pass completion from Kinnick to Green was the last play of the first quarter.

The second quarter began slowly with the two teams exchanging punts and the Hawkeyes began a drive with the ball on the South Dakota 46-yard line. It didn't take long for the Hawks to move the ball down the field, with Kinnick scoring a touchdown on a run around left end. His perfect drop-kick made the score 14-0.

South Dakota could not overcome the stiff Iowa defense and was again forced to punt the ball away. By sending in fresh players, they forced Iowa to punt also. But each time the Hawkeyes punted, Kinnick consistently kicked the ball out of bounds just in front of the Coyote goal line. (Just like he and Frank Carideo had practiced.)

On one of Taplett's long punts, Kinnick made a good return to the South Dakota 35-yard line where he lateraled the ball to Busk for an additional thirteen yards. On the next play, Busk went around left end for another nine yards to the thirteen. Kinnick then ran around right end for a touchdown. With another good drop-kick, the score was 21-0.

Once again, after receiving the kick-off, the Coyotes punted.

Taplett boomed a kick to the Iowa 33-yard line and Kinnick could manage only a five yard return. On the first play from scrimmage, Kinnick launched a long pass to Busk who caught the ball on the South Dakota 30-yard line and raced the rest of the way for a touchdown. The drop-kick, again good by Kinnick, made the half-time score Iowa 28-South Dakota 0.

Anderson started his second team in the second half. Henry Vollenweider waited for the kick-off from Wernli. The Dubuque native took the ball on his own 10-yard line and outran everybody—ninety yards for a touchdown. The Iowa fans and bench were in a frenzy. Roger Pettit missed the extra point attempt, but nobody seemed to notice. The Hawks had a 34-0 shutout going.

The Coyotes were not yet ready to call it quits. With Burns and Taplett as the work horses, South Dakota drove the ball down to the Iowa 41-yard line. A surprise pass from Taplett to Solberg was good to the 24-yard line. Back on the ground, Burns, Taplett, and Wernli plunged through the line little by little until the ball was on the Hawkeye nine. Burns made a gain of six on third down. But the Iowa defense denied the fourth down attempt at a score and took over.

The teams, with many reserves in the game at this point, could gain no advantage and exchanged punts. Iowa got the ball back its own five. Jack McKinnon made a run of twenty yards. Roger Pettit attempted a pass which was intercepted by South Dakota's Kessler on the Iowa 28-yard line. On the next play the tables were turned when Buzz Dean intercepted Taplett's pass on the twenty-five.

Jack McKinnon got the ball again and was on his way to a good gain when Petranek, South Dakota's left tackle, grabbed the ball out of his hands. The Coyotes took over in Iowa territory, but could make no headway and Taplett punted the ball out of bounds on the Iowa 7-yard line as the third quarter came to a close.

The first part of the final quarter was a struggle for advantage during which neither team could move. Finally, the Coyotes were able to put together a sustained drive and got as far as the Iowa

15-yard line where they fumbled. Joseph Moore alertly recovered for the Hawks.

It was now Iowa's turn at a drive. The passing of Buzz Dean and runs by McLain, Dean, and Couppee moved the ball down to the South Dakota 20-yard line. But there the drive ran out of steam. The Hawks were called for offside, then Dean was sacked for a 12-yard loss. A fourth down pass from Dean to McLain was complete, but inches short of a first down.

Both defenses stiffened as the game wound down. Iowa got the ball on the South Dakota 40-yard line when Al Couppee recovered a Coyote fumble. With less than a minute left in the game, Kinnick replaced Dean in the backfield and John Maher replaced Moore at end.

Kinnick passed to Maher who caught the ball on the South Dakota 15-yard line. Kinnick then found Robert Kelley in the end zone and completed the pass for Iowa's sixth touchdown. Kinnick's fifth dropkick of the day was good and the game ended: Iowa 41-South Dakota 0.

The Hawkeyes were winners, and for the first time at home since October of 1937. Almost everyone had gotten to play. Kinnick had shown everyone that his ankle was truly healed. He had carried the ball eight times for 110 yards and three touchdowns (one a 65-yard run). He had also thrown two touchdown passes and drop-kicked five extra points. His twenty-three point sole effort was the best for Iowa since Nanny Pape's four touchdowns in 1928.

The offense, limited to mostly off-tackle plays and end runs, had accumulated almost 300 yards. Russ Busk had five carries for forty-three yards; Al Couppee had thirty-nine yards on four carries; and Jack McKinnon had carried twice for twenty-five yards.

The line had done a superb job of opening holes—especially big Hank Luebcke who had been scoffed at by a couple of Purdue scouts before the game. They weren't so doubtful after seeing him in action. They hadn't seen much of the Iowa offense, either. But the fans had seen plenty of football.

The Hawkeyes had gained 150 yards in the air, completing

seven out of seventeen passes, with one interception. The Coyotes had completed two out of ten passes with two interceptions. The punters had gotten a good workout with a combined total of twenty-three punts. The Hawkeyes had dominated on the returns, however, making 131 yards to the Coyotes 23.

*Al Couppee, quarterback
(courtesy: University of Iowa Archives)*

Al Couppee recalled the thrill of that first victory: "We found out we could win and make it work." The fans had been treated to quite a show. A writer for the Iowa City newspaper said, "It's going to be mighty interesting watching Eddie Anderson's first Hawkeye team. Before November 25th, the boys may set an all-time high for gridiron entertainment in these parts." He didn't realize how close to the truth that statement was.

There were, however, the skeptics—those who thought the victory was a fluke, or those who pointed out " . . . after all, it wasn't exactly a conference game." The *New York Times* reported the game in a two inch summary at the bottom of one of the many sports pages, next to the trap shooting scores. They did report the three touchdowns and five drop-kicks by "a stocky senior back" named Nile Kinnick.

But it was a tremendous start—the best in a long time for the Hawkeyes. The real test would come in the first conference game—the following week against Indiana.

# CHAPTER 5

# INDIANA: FIRST CONFERENCE GAME

Saturday, October 7th, was Dad's Day in Iowa City. The weather was unseasonably hot and windy. By game time, the temperature on the playing field would equal that of a bright summer afternoon: 90 + degrees.

The Hawkeyes, in spite of their 41-0 blasting of South Dakota, could hardly be considered favorites. There had not been an Iowa victory over Indiana since 1921. Also, Iowa football teams were famous for their lack of success in Big Ten opening games. There had been only two such victories since 1900, and no conference home victory at all since 1933.

Following the big victory over South Dakota, there was a lot of activity on the Iowa campus the week before the Indiana game. In order to protect his players from all the distractions, Eddie Anderson sequestered the entire squad on Friday night, putting them up in a quiet ward of the University Hospital. It was one of the perks he enjoyed from being a doctor on staff in the urology department.

The Hoosiers, coached by "Bo" McMillin, were big, strong, and fast with a lot of talent. They had a terrific passer named Harold Hursh and a pair of strong ball carriers in Zimmer and Tofil. The line included Archie Harris, who, later, would hold the world discus record. Another fine lineman was Emil "Moose"

Uremovich, who would one day play for the Detroit Lions. Fifty years later, he recalled, "How well I remember the Iowa-Indiana game of 1939. It was so hot that I lost about twenty pounds, and didn't recover until Monday of the following week."

*Iowa Stadium on Game Day—Indiana (author's collection)*

Iowa's starting lineup was the same as the South Dakota game. The opposition would be much tougher than the previous week.

Iowa won the toss and Captain Prasse, due to the strong wind, elected to defend the south goal. His kick-off sailed far over the Indiana goal line and the ball was put in play on the 20-yard line. Three straight line plunges by Tofil moved the ball to the Indiana 32-yard line and a first down. Taking the ball for the fourth time, he skirted around left end. When hit at the 40-yard line, he pitched to Zimmer, who ran out of bounds after gaining three more yards. Zimmer got the next call and was crunched by Jim Walker for a loss of a yard. Zimmer was hit so hard he called time out, but stayed in the game.

With the Iowa line stiffening, Hursh decided to take to the air and fired a long pass to the recovered Zimmer, who caught the ball on the Hawkeye 35-yard line, broke several tackles and made it to the eighteen. It was Iowa's turn to call a time out.

When play resumed, it was Zimmer again—this time around left end for an eleven-yard gain. But here the Hawkeye defense solidified. After a couple of foiled scoring attempts, Herbert kicked an Indiana field goal and the Hoosiers were on the scoreboard 3-0.

Emil Uremovich, following his team's score, ran the length of the field, passing the Iowa team, singing Iowa's "Corn Song." This taunt added insult to injury and the Hawks were determined to get the points back.

The Hoosier kick-off was taken by Nile Kinnick, who made a twenty-five yard return to his own 40-yard line, where he lateralled to Russ Busk. The "Rabbit" was able to get to the Indian 30-yard line before being dragged down by Hursh. Runs by Busk and Green moved the ball to the Indiana 25-yard line, but here the drive ended and the Hoosiers took over on downs.

Tofil made a first down on a ten-yard gain, and Hursh tried another pass, this time to Harris. Although the pass was incomplete, Busk was called for pass interference and the ball was placed on the Iowa forty-three.

Herbert and Brooks tried unsuccessfully to crack the Iowa defensive line, so Hursh took to the air again. This time he found Zimmer, who had slipped behind the secondary and caught the ball for a gain of twenty yards. Brooks, on a fake pass play, ran around right end for a touchdown. Herbert place-kicked the extra point, making the score 10-0.

Uremovich let loose with another chorus of the "Corn Song," which really burned the Hawkeyes, including Al Couppee who said, "I was just stung, and was ready to kill that so and so."

Kinnick took the kick-off and made a return of twenty yards to his own 25-yard line. With a change in strategy, Kinnick quick-kicked on the next play. The ball went seventy-three yards to the Indiana 3-yard line.

The Hoosiers could not move the ball and were forced to punt. Kinnick received the ball on the Indiana 40-yard line, juggled it a little, then ran to the thirty before being stopped. On the first play, Kinnick went back to throw and found Erwin Prasse in the clear. The Hawkeye end caught the ball on the 9-yard line and ran it in for a touchdown. The margin was narrowed to 10-7 when Kinnick drop kicked the extra point.

A few of the Iowa players ran by Moose Uremovich, singing "Indiana, My Indiana."

The first quarter ended with no additional scoring and with the Hoosiers in possession on their own twenty.

Max Hawkins went into the game for Henry Luebcke and Ray Murphy replaced Bill Green at fullback. Indiana could make only one first down (on a penalty) and Bringle punted. Kinnick returned the ball to his own 42-yard line after a gain of seven yards.

On the first play, Kinnick, running off right tackle, broke into the clear and dashed fifty-five yards to the Indiana 3-yard line. On the next play, he smashed over left tackle for a touchdown behind a crushing block by Jim Walker. Kinnick drop-kicked the extra point and Iowa had the lead 14-10.

The Hoosiers returned the kick-off to their own 28-yard line, but could advance no further, due to blistering hits by Enich and Hawkins. Indiana was compelled to punt and Kinnick returned the ball down the sideline just beyond mid-field, getting by one defender with the use of a stiff-arm.

After a gain of six yards, Kinnick dropped back to pass, but slipped and fell at the mid-field stripe. But the young halfback was unshaken and on the next play went back to throw again. He found Prasse, who had beaten Maddox near the goal line. The ball was thrown perfectly and Prasse made a spectacular over-the shoulder catch, and ran into the end zone, never breaking stride.

Kinnick's perfect record of completed drop-kicks ended as the kick went wide. It was Iowa 20-Indiana 10.

Tofil made a fine return of the kick-off to his own 43-yard line. Passes from McGuire to Dumke and Tofil advanced the ball to the Iowa 38-yard line. A third pass was incomplete, but an interference call against Iowa placed the ball on the Hawkeye 14-yard line. Hursh's pass to Dumke was good for six more yards.

Following two more unsuccessful pass attempts, Hursh found Tipmore, a reserve, open in the end zone and fired the ball to him for the touchdown. Tofil's extra point made it Iowa 20-Indiana 17.

The Hawkeyes wanted desperately to score once more before halftime. Kinnick received the kick-off near his own goal line. Just before being hit at the 25-yard line, he lateralled to Gilleard who made seven more yards.

On first down, Murphy smashed over center for a gain of ten yards. On the next play, he gained sixteen yards, but the play was called back because of a holding penalty. Kinnick tried a pass, but the ball was intercepted by Hursh near mid-field. Just before going down, Hursh pitched to Smith who managed to get to the Iowa 29-yard line. Chuck Tollefson was injured on the play and was replaced by Luebcke.

Hursh took to the air again. After two incompletions, and a short gain of six yards, Hursh's pass was intercepted by Kinnick at the Indiana 20-yard line.

Gilleard ran for a few yards, followed by a gain of sixteen by Kinnick. A long desperation pass fell incomplete as the first half ended: Iowa 20-Indiana 17.

The Hawks were able to enjoy their slim lead while they tried to recover from the terrible heat. Although there were the normal strains and bruises, the overall condition of the team was good. There was no feeling of letting up. Jim Walker, who had been up against Archie Harris the entire first half, was determined to finish the battle after the intermission. As they left the locker room for the second half, the heat and humidity hit them in the face, even more stifling than before. It would be a brutal second half. None of the 20,000 fans had left. They were anxious for more action and a Hawkeye victory.

White, for Indiana, kicked off to start the second half. The temperature seemed even higher than before. Kinnick received the kick near his own goal and made a return of thirty-three yards. But the Indiana defensive line was rock solid. The Hawkeyes were forced to punt and Kinnick kicked deep to Hursh, who made a return of eleven yards before being dropped by Ham

Snider. The Hoosiers started with good field position on their own 34-yard line.

Tofil plunged over right tackle for two yards just to keep Iowa's defensive line "honest." On the next play, Hursh fired a pass to Harris, who was finally forced out of bounds on the Iowa 37-yard line. Jim Walker told Al Couppee, who was playing linebacker behind him, that he (Walker) was going to "really take care" of Harris. Zimmer took the ball over right tackle on the next play for two yards. Couppee recalled, "I heard an awful smash and there were those two guys [Walker and Harris] really going at it."

On the next play, Hursh let the ball fly and Zimmer made a great over-the-shoulder catch at the Hawkeye 15-yard line, and outran Kinnick and Murphy into the end zone for a touchdown. Herbert's extra point was blocked and the score became Indiana 23-Iowa 20.

White kicked off again to Kinnick on the goal line. Nile fumbled the ball, but it was recovered by Iowa on their own thirteen. Two attempts by Kinnick over right tackle gained seven yards. On the second play, Al Couppee suffered a separated shoulder while blocking Harris. He was replaced at quarterback by Gallagher.

On third down, Kinnick quick-kicked, but the ball went only as far as the Iowa 39-yard line. Tofil got the call for the Hoosiers and moved the ball eleven yards. Hursh tried a pass to Harris, but Russ Busk broke up the play. The next attempt, however, succeeded and Harris was tackled on the Hawkeye 12-yard line. Runs by Zimmer and Tofil advanced the ball to the five. Hursh went back to pass and found his secondary receiver, Rucinski, in the end zone. The pass was complete for a touchdown. Tofil attempted the extra point, but the kick was blocked. The score was Indiana 29-Iowa 20.

Buzz Dean replaced Busk in the backfield. White's kick-off went to Kinnick who returned the ball to his own 23-yard line. Once again the Hoosier defensive line toughened to the Iowa runners. Kinnick's punt went to Zimmer who made a return of nine yards to his own 44-yard line. Zimmer was injured on the play and was replaced by Smith.

Dumke tried to pierce the Iowa line, but was thrown for a loss of four yards by Bill Green, who had just come in for Ray Murphy. Hursh went back to the air and tossed a first down strike to Dumke in Iowa territory. Dumke was injured and replaced by Brooks. Another first down pass, this time from Hursh to Smith, moved the ball to the Iowa 32-yard line as the third quarter ended.

*William Green, fullback (courtesy: University of Iowa Archives)*

As the teams switched directions for the final quarter, it was clear that the heat was beginning to take its toll. Henry Luebcke had come out of the game with an abdominal injury of an uncertain nature. He was taken to the hospital where it was discovered he had suffered a severe hernia. The doctors operated immediately. Luebcke would never play again. Later, the doctors said that if it had not been for Luebcke's weight-loss and conditioning (ordered by Anderson), they would not have been able to save his life.

The fourth quarter started with Herbert returning to the game as the Hoosier quarterback. On a first down pass attempt to Bringle, the ball was intercepted by Bill Diehl who made a return to the Iowa 27-yard line.

Now it was the Hawkeyes' turn to launch an aerial attack. After an unsuccessful attempt to Prasse, Kinnick fired a shot to Buzz Dean for a first down. Back on the ground, Green gained seven yards on two successive smashes over right tackle and Dean moved the ball nearly to mid-field on a run over left tackle. Prasse, who had shifted to the backfield, made seven yards around right end.

Bill Green and Nile Kinnick alternated off-tackle runs, moving to the Indiana 19-yard line. Buzz Dean made six more on an end run to the left. The Hoosier line was beginning to wear down. Prasse made ten yards on an end-around play before being stopped by Tofil.

Buzz Dean made a first down off tackle to the three. On the next play, Green went up the middle and blasted through for a touchdown. Kinnick's extra point attempt missed, but the margin had been narrowed: Indiana 29-Iowa 26.

Dean kicked off to Indiana's Herbert who fielded the ball on his own 5-yard line and made a return of seventeen. On a one-yard plunge by Smith, Mike Enich, who had played the entire game without rest, collapsed. Wally Bergstrom replaced him. Enich was taken to the hospital where he was revived, suffering dehydration from the intense heat.

*Mike Enich, tackle (courtesy: University of Iowa Archives)*

Hursh went back to the air. His first pass was intercepted by a high leap by Bill Green on the Indiana 31-yard line.

Kinnick made seventeen yards and a first down by cutting inside the right end. In the traditional Kinnick style, he faked out the defensive end by twisting his hips, leaving the defender clutching only air.

From the 10-yard line, Dean tried left end with no success. Kinnick's second down pass to Gallagher was incomplete. On third down, Kinnick tried it himself around right end, but was thrown for a loss of five yards. It was fourth down with not much time left. A field goal would tie the game.

Emil Uremovich recalled, "Iowa had the ball on our 20-yard line and could have kicked a field goal to tie us. I heard Kinnick give some guy hell and said he was calling the play." Kinnick is quoted as saying to his teammates, "Forget the tie—we're going all the way!"

Nile dropped back to pass and spotted Prasse in the end zone and let the ball fly. The pass seemed out of reach, but the three-sport star grabbed it with his fingertips and held on for the touchdown. Kinnick missed the extra point attempt, but Iowa had regained the lead 32-29.

Uremovich remembered, "It seemed like every time we went ahead of Iowa and thought it was won, they would come back." Now it was Indiana's turn to try to come back. Henry Vollenweider went in for Gallagher and Buzz Dean kicked off to Hursh. He pitched out to Zimmer, but he could only reach the 19-yard line. With only a few seconds left to play, the Indiana drive was stopped by a nearly-exhausted Iowa defense. Kinnick kept the ball on the ground to use up the final seconds.

It was over and the Hawkeyes had overcome the jinx of Big Ten openers. They had come from behind twice in Eddie Anderson's conference initiation. The fans were overjoyed and the sportswriters impressed. George Stickler, writing for the *Chicago Tribune* said, "The Renaissance arrived at Iowa today, borne triumphantly on the shoulders of Nile Kinnick and fleet-footed Erwin Prasse."

It had indeed been an impressive performance. The total offense was fairly equal for both teams: Iowa with 325 yards and Indiana with 362. The Hawkeyes had excelled with 222 yards rushing to the Hoosiers' 163. Indiana had dominated the total passing yardage 227 to 109, but the Hawkeye passes had come in clutch situations. Kinnick's average punting yardage of forty-two was ten better than Indiana's; Kinnick had also accumulated 171 yards in kick-off returns.

Eddie Anderson had used 23 players on this steamy afternoon. It was the most he would use in a game for the rest of the season. Iowa had finally ended the 18-year drought of losses to Indiana and finally had a Big Ten win at a conference home opener.

Although celebration was in order, the Hawks had to count

their injuries and get ready for mighty Michigan the following week. Luebcke was out and Couppee was a questionable starter. They would need everyone healthy for the upcoming battle in Ann Arbor—the first road trip.

# CHAPTER 6

## MICHIGAN: FIRST ROAD TRIP

The weather was perfect for football in Ann Arbor on Saturday, October 14th, 1939. The bright sun highlighted the red and gold maple leaves around the stadium. There was a crisp tanginess of autumn in the air as the crowd of 27,512 filed into their seats.

Coach H.O. "Fritz" Crisler's Wolverines were, like Iowa, unbeaten thus far in the season. They also had their share of injuries. Paul Kromer, the "Touchdown Twin" of Tom Harmon in the Michigan backfield, had not yet recovered from an injury sustained the previous week in the victory over Michigan State. Harmon, known as the "Hoosier Hammer," because of his Gary, Indiana, roots, would have to do double duty.

Michigan was a team full of talent. Ed Frutig, the big left end, and Robert Westfall, the fullback, were both quick and tough to bring down. The Wolverine captain was quarterback Forest Evashevski, who was considered the team's best blocker and sure-handed pass receiver. This was the same man who would later lead the Hawkeyes to success as head coach. Also a member of the team was Bob Flora, who would later travel with "Evy" to Iowa City as an assistant coach.

Flora recalled that everyone on the Michigan team "respected Nile Kinnick as a great triple threat." So much that most of the practice time the previous week was spent on plays designed to stop Kinnick. The Wolverines knew they would have to be at their best against the Hawkeyes. Evashevski remembered that Iowa's strength was "unity, hustle, and perfection" and that "it was a team that rallied around Kinnick."

*Forest Evashevski, Michigan captain and future Iowa football coach/athletic director (courtesy: University of Iowa Archives)*

The Hawks were as ready as they could be. Tollefson and Enich were back to form following a week's rest. Hank Luebcke, of course, was gone and was replaced in the starting line up by Ham Snider. Al Couppee, wearing a "horse collar" neck brace, would start, but was not a hundred percent. Anderson needed his field general in action if at all possible. Buzz Dean took over the right halfback position and Jens Norgaard started at right end and did the place-kicking. Other than that, the line up was the same as the previous games.

Iowa won the toss and requested the ball. Harmon kicked off for Michigan to his rival, Kinnick, who made the return to his own 27-yard line. Runs by Bill Green and Kinnick could not produce a first down, so Kinnick punted.

Michigan was no more successful in running attempts by Harmon and Westfall. Smith punted back to the Hawkeyes and the ball rolled out of bounds on the Iowa 22-yard line.

Green, on a reverse play, made three yards and Buzz Dean got four more off tackle. On third down, Kinnick faded back and launched a pass to Dean, who gathered the ball in on the Michigan 40-yard line and outdistanced everybody to the end zone for a touchdown. Kinnick's perfect drop-kick made the score: Iowa 7-Michigan 0. The Michigan fans were silent.

Jens Norgaard's kick-off carried out of the end zone and the Wolverines started from their own 20-yard line. After two short gains by Westfall, Trosko quick-kicked to the Hawkeye 36-yard line.

Neither team could sustain a drive, so Kinnick and Smith put on a punting exhibition. Finally, Smith got off a short punt that looked as if it would give Iowa good field position. But Kinnick's sure hands failed him and he fumbled the ball. Savilla for Michigan recovered it on the Iowa 40-yard line and it was the Wolverines who had the advantage.

After an incomplete pass attempt and a short gain by Harmon on a fake pass, Frutig grabbed a Harmon toss on the Iowa 10-yard line and lumbered to the two where Kinnick pushed him out of bounds. On first down, Westfall tried to dive over center, but Tollefson stopped him cold. On second down, Harmon ran through a big hole at left guard and scored the touchdown standing up. Harmon's place kick for the extra point tied the score at seven.

Buzz Dean took Harmon's kick-off on his own 22-yard line and made eight yards before being tackled by Rogers. On an end run to the left, Dean made it to the Iowa 44-yard line for a first down. Successive runs by Kinnick and Green netted only three yards. On third down, Kinnick fired a pass to Green who made it to the Michigan 29-yard line, where he was stopped by Harmon and Kodros.

*Herman "Ham" Snider, guard (courtesy: University of Iowa Archives)*

Kinnick tried a run through the line, but found no openings. Iowa was charged five yards on a delay of game penalty, and Kinnick tried a desperation pass to Dean, but the ball fell incomplete as the first quarter ended.

On the first play of the second quarter, Buzz Dean burst through the line with a gain of fourteen yards to the Michigan 20-yard line, just short of a first down. The Hawkeyes gambled on fourth down and Bill Green made the necessary yardage. Two more runs by Green moved the ball to the Michigan 12-yard line. A third down pass attempt was knocked down by Harmon and Trosko. On fourth and five, Kinnick's pass (thrown under heavy pressure) to Prasse was intercepted in the end zone by Harmon. Later, Kinnick would say, "They came in faster [the pass rush] than any team I have ever played."

From his own 20-yard line, Harmon ran for seven yards around left end. On the next play, Trosko tried a reverse, but was tripped up by Jim Walker for a loss of five.

The ball changed hands a few times due to sloppy play by both teams: an Iowa fumble, a Michigan pass intercepted. Another long return of a Kinnick punt by Trosko moved the ball to the Iowa 26-yard line.

Harmon ran off-tackle for eleven yards. Then, on the next play, he threw a flat pass to Evashevski who made it to the 4-yard line before being tackled by Green. Westfall made two more yards over center. Then, starting to his left, Harmon cut back and lunged through left guard and scored. He missed the attempt at the extra point, but the Wolverines had a 13-7 lead.

Bill Gallagher replaced Al Couppee, whose shoulder could not take any more, at quarterback. Kinnick now called the offensive plays. It was a little tough on Gallagher as he would have to play Couppee's linebacker position on defense when he was better suited to the secondary.

Kinnick returned Harmon's kick-off twenty-two yards to the Iowa 27-yard line. Runs by Kinnick and Green and an incomplete pass to Jens Norgaard forced the Hawkeyes to punt on fourth down. Somehow, Savilla was able to sneak through and block Kinnick's kick, the only one he would have blocked all season. Iowa recovered on the 37-yard line, but it was short of the first down and the Wolverines took over again with good field position.

Harmon, behind crushing blocks by Evashevski & Co., raced round left end to the Iowa 8-yard line. Jens Norgaard recalled, "Being blocked by Evashevski was like being kicked by a mule." On the next lay, Harmon ran the same play to the right and scored his third touchdown of the day. His extra point kick was good and made the score Michigan 20-Iowa 7.

Kinnick was able to return Harmon's kick-off to the Iowa 24-

yard line, but that was as far as the Hawkeyes could get. The first half ended with Michigan's Melzow dropping Kinnick for a ten-yard loss.

Eddie Anderson was forced to make some changes for the second half. Bill Diehl and Jim Walker were out with injuries. Bruno Andruska got the call to replace Diehl at center. Wally Bergstrom (who hadn't even played football except as a freshman and a few days the following fall before classes started) replaced Walker at left tackle. "I didn't know some of the plays," Bergstrom recalled. "Heck, I was so new I didn't even know some of our players."

**Wallace Bergstrom, tackle (courtesy: University of Iowa Archives)**

Jerry Ankeny would play for the injured Couppee with Kinnick continuing to call the plays. Ed McLain started the second half at the right halfback position. The Hawks were beat up, but not yet beaten.

Harmon kicked off to start the second half. Kinnick received the ball on his own 6-yard line and made a twenty-seven yard return before being downed by Frutig.

After two unsuccessful runs through the line, Kinnick completed a pass to McLain, but the play was short of the first down. Kinnick punted and the ball rolled out of bounds on the Michigan 29-yard line.

Harmon got the first call and broke three tackles before being stopped by Mike Enich after a gain of seven yards. Harmon made another yard on the next play off tackle. Westfall plunged through the line to the Michigan 39-yard line for the first down.

An end run by Harmon was good for seven yards, but the Wolverines were penalized for holding and the ball was moved back to the Michigan 21-yard line. Trosko tried to slip around the end, but Bill Green shot through and tackled him for a loss of a few yards. Another Michigan penalty moved the ball back to the 2-yard line.

Smith's punt from his own end zone, under a heavy rush, went only sixteen yards before rolling out of bounds. Iowa had good field position and was threatening at last. On the first play, Kinnick went back to pass and spotted Jerry Ankeny in the end zone. He let the ball go, but Harmon snatched the pass on the 10-yard line and scampered ninety yards for a touchdown. His successful extra point made the score Michigan 27-Iowa 7.

Ed McLain returned Harmon's kick-off to the Iowa thirty. Kinnick, Green, and McLain each tried to pierce the Wolverine line with no success. Evashevski and Kodros were making great individual defensive plays. Evy recalled, "We were able to outman the Hawks and beat them with freshness."

After an exchange of punts, Iowa had the ball on their own 25. The Wolverine defense would not yield. McLain tried a spinner over center for no gain. Green was tackled by Evashevski for a loss of two yards. Kinnick lost seven on another great effort by Evashevski. Kinnick later wrote, "They overshifted a man and a half on the strong side and bottled up completely all my running plays." Just like they had practiced it all week.

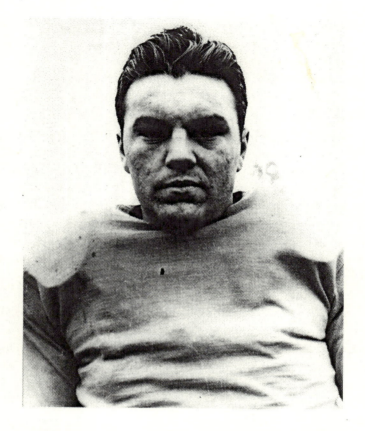

*Gerald Ankeny, back (courtesy: University of Iowa Archives)*

Michigan got the ball back near midfield after Kinnick punted. Harmon burst through the line off tackle to the Iowa 39-yard line and a first down. Evashevski recalled, "Couppee, Prasse, Murphy, Enich, et al were good players, but when one was injured, we ran at his replacement."

Harmon tried a pass to Evashevski, but Kinnick intercepted the ball and stepped out of bounds on his own twenty-eight. But the Hawks could not make the necessary yardage for a first down and Kinnick punted as the third quarter ended. Trosko received the punt, but slipped and fell on his own 28-yard line.

The fourth quarter was similar to the third, except neither

team could score. The Hawkeyes, many playing in unfamiliar positions, could not move the ball. Crisler sent in many fresh substitutes who put up a strong pass defense, but the Iowa defense would not bend, either. On the final play of the game, Kinnick tried a long pass to Gilleard that was tipped into the air and intercepted by Christy as the gun sounded. It ended Michigan 27-Iowa 7.

Tom Harmon had scored all of the Wolverine points, either by touchdown or place kicking. Bob Flora remembered, "Harmon had a great day, but the key was that we shut down Iowa's kicking game. Our punt returns killed Iowa."

Al Couppee said, "We led in most of the departments of play yards gained, first downs—surprisingly, we outplayed Michigan in the ball game. We just couldn't get the ball across the goal line and they were hot as a firecracker. It was unfortunate we had to play Michigan at that point in the season. If it had been anybody but Michigan that week, I think we'd have gone unbeaten that season."

Statistically, the quarterback was right. The teams were almost even in first downs, punts, and rushing yardage. The Hawkeyes wound up with 125 more yards passing and 100 more total yards than the Wolverines, but Michigan had come out on top in the only statistic that really counts—total points.

Some of the Iowa fans lost confidence in the Hawks and figured the Indiana game had been just a fluke after all. But the players, though physically hurt and mentally disappointed, were not ready to lose faith in themselves.

In a letter to his parents, Nile Kinnick wrote, "I am disgusted with the game I played. Michigan had a fine team with a very good back by the name of Harmon. He is not as good as we made him look and we are not as poor as the score indicates." Concerning Eddie Anderson, Nile said, " . . . I wish we could play it over . . . it breaks my heart to have sort of let him down." He was not the only one who felt that way about their head coach.

Nile's father, in an answer to his son's letter, said, "It takes a better man to be outstanding in defeat than in victory" and he told Nile to bounce back.

Anderson also knew the importance of bouncing back. He told the team: "Let's leave this game here in Ann Arbor. We're going to stay over in Chicago tonight, and we're going to see the Chicago Bears/Green Bay Packers game in Wrigley Field tomorrow. Forget this football game and let's have some fun tonight." Anderson wanted his players to relax a little. Al Couppee recalled, "It was a masterful piece of football coaching psychology."

Anderson knew that the sooner they could put the Michigan game behind them, the sooner they could start preparing for the next one. It would be tough—physically and mentally—getting ready for the next contest, another away game, this time at Wisconsin.

# CHAPTER 7

## WISCONSIN: REBOUND

Anderson had two weeks to get his Hawkeyes back on track. The open date on the Saturday between the Michigan and Wisconsin road trips gave the players much-needed time to heal the injuries, both mental and physical.

Nile Kinnick wrote to his parents, "My desire to do well is as good as it ever was, but any personal ambition as to recognition following the season has pretty much gone out of my mind. Nothing but carelessness and thoughtlessness made me play the game I did at Michigan. I trust that it won't happen again." Although the sensitive tailback was being a little hard on himself, his statement pretty much reflected the feelings shared by teammates. They were down, but far from out.

Anderson used the first of the two weeks to take a look at some of his reserve players. He tried out many of them who had not, up to now, played very much in order to see who might be realistic substitutes for the starters, should any more go down in a game. The freshman team was called in to run scrimmages against a team made up of players such as: Matt Miletich, John Maher, Carl Conrad, Oops Gilleard, Hank Vollenweider, Bill Gallagher, Jerry Ankeny, and others who the coaches wanted to look at. In the end, though, it was clear to Anderson that while the reserves worked valiantly, the small band of current starters would have to bear the brunt of the playing time.

Some changes were made in the starting lineup—some due to injury and some to strategy. Wally Bergstrom, in his first start, would be the left tackle in place of Jim Walker, whose knee was seriously injured. Bill Diehl, though not a hundred percent due to being hurt in the Michigan game, would start at center. Max Hawkins would be the right guard. Mike Enich and Chuck Tollefson would be ready at their regular positions of right tackle and left guard respectively.

Couppee, wearing his shoulder brace, was ready for action at quarterback. Kinnick, McLain, and Murphy rounded out the starting backfield. On the strategic side, Anderson decided to start Fred Smith and Jens Norgaard, two tough hitters, at the end positions. Prasse and Evans were ready for later action.

The traveling squad was an unheard of total of twenty-six players. When asked about this small group, Anderson replied that they would just have to be "iron men." Sportswriters, including Bert McGrane, picked up on the term and the "Ironmen" label was born.

The team took the Rock Island Rocket to Chicago where they worked out at Stagg Stadium at the University of Chicago, then took another train north to Milwaukee, spending the night in the Shrader Hotel. The next morning it was another train ride west to Madison.

There were 21,000 Dad's Day fans at Camp Randall Stadium in Madison, Wisconsin. The Hawkeyes had not won there in ten years. The Badgers, though winless in Big Ten play so far, were a talented team. They were coached by Harry Stuhldreher, who had quarterbacked Knute Rockne's Notre Dame team as one of the famous "Four Horsemen." He had two outstanding backs in George Paskvan and Tony Gradisnik, along with a strong line. The Hawkeyes had their work cut out for them.

Iowa won the toss and Kinnick, who was the acting captain, elected to kick. Jens Norgaard's kick went to Gradisnik, who made a return of ten yards to his own 23-yard line.

On the first play from scrimmage, Paskvan ran for nine yards. On the next play, he picked up the first down with a gain of six. The third play was Paskvan again, but this time he was stopped after two yards by Diehl and Norgaard. Subsequent running attempts by York and Paskvan failed to achieve the first down yardage and the Badgers had to punt.

Fred Gage's kick went to Kinnick who caught the ball on his own 20-yard line, but was dropped immediately by Eckl. The Hawks' attempt at breaking Wisconsin's defensive line was not successful. Runs by Kinnick and Murphy were good for a total of only three yards.

Kinnick's punt went to Gradisnik. He returned the ball five yards to his own 45-yard line, where he was stopped by Norgaard, who was hurt on the play, but stayed in the game.

The back-and-forth action continued through two series of plays with neither team gaining an advantage. On an Iowa punt, Gradisnik returned the ball almost to midfield where he was again tackled by Norgaard. Fifty years later, the scrappy end recalled, "The first time I laid into him, I felt pretty groggy, but after the second time, I really didn't know where I was. I was staggering around out there and Anderson sent Evans in for me and he did a beautiful job." It was the last time Jens Norgaard would ever play football.

*Jens Norgaard, end (courtesy: University of Iowa Archives))*

After a no-gain running play, the Badgers decided to take to the air. Gradisnik went back to pass for the first time. The throw was intercepted by Kinnick on his own 22-yard line. Once again, however, the Hawkeyes failed to gain a first down and had to punt the ball away. Gradisnik made an eleven-yard return to the Wisconsin 37-yard line.

On a smash over center, Gradisnik made ten yards and a first down. The next play was identical with identical results. A surprise pass from Gradisnik to Lorenz moved the ball to the Iowa fourteen. After trying another running play, for no gain, Gradisnik fired a pass to Fred Gage, who made a sensational catch in the end zone for a touchdown. Gage's successful place-kick for the extra point made the score Wisconsin 7-Iowa 0.

Including the Michigan game, the Hawkeyes had now allowed thirty-four unanswered points.

Gage's kick-off went to Kinnick who took the ball on his own 10-yard line and cut and wove his way through the defense for a fifty-five yard return. Gradisnik, the last defender, dragged him down on the Wisconsin 35-yard line. Bill Diehl was hurt on the play and Bruno Andruska took over at center. Bill Green and Russ Busk came into the game for Ray Murphy and Ed McLain in the backfield.

On the first play, Green tried a pitch-out to Busk, but the play lost two yards. After an incomplete pass attempt, Kinnick threw to Green for a gain of seven yards. Wisconsin was offside, but the penalty still left the Hawks short as the first quarter ended.

Cone replaced Gradisnik as the second quarter began. On fourth down, Kinnick completed a pass over the middle to Couppee, who was tackled on the Wisconsin 15-yard line for a first down. Bill Green made three more over center. Prasse, in the game for Smith, tried an end-around play, but lost two yards. Green's off-tackle run got the two yards back, but Iowa was penalized five yards for illegal motion. Kinnick dropped back to pass and found Couppee in the end zone for a touchdown. Kinnick's drop-kick was too low and the score was Wisconsin 7-Iowa 6.

Cone received Prasse's kick-off on his own five and raced up the sideline to the 35-yard line where Russ Busk pushed him out of bounds. The Badgers, with Paskvan smashing through the Iowa line and Cone completing passes, were able to put together a sustained drive. However, they fell short when Kinnick knocked down a Cone pass. McLain and Murphy were sent in to beef up the defense. Two plays later, Peterson punted for Wisconsin and the ball rolled out of bounds on the Iowa ten.

For the rest of the first half, the two teams battled for an advantage that neither could obtain. On one play, Kinnick made a 54-yard gain, but it was nullified because he had thrown a forward pass as he was being tackled. Kinnick also intercepted one of Cone's passes, but the Hawkeyes could not capitalize on the turnover. The first half ended Wisconsin 7-Iowa 6.

*Max Hawkins, guard (courtesy: University of Iowa Archives)*

Each team had been conservative in its first half of play, much to the surprise of the fans and sportswriters. The Badgers had discovered they could run with success—especially at some of the non-veteran Hawkeye players. Wally Berstrom, playing in his first starting role, remembered, "Frank Carideo used to say that Paskvan set a record that day—for most yards gained over one position—me." Al Couppee, playing behind Bergstrom at linebacker agreed, "I never got so much business as a linebacker in any game I ever played." But Bergstrom and the rest of the Iowa defense had held Wisconsin when it had counted—on the critical plays preventing first downs—and had forced turnovers.

During the intermission, Anderson told the team that they had to do a better job hustling down the field to cover punts—that nobody was getting to the punt receivers. Ham Snider later asked Jens Norgaard why he didn't jump up and say something since he had made two grueling tackles on punt receivers. Norgaard replied, "Ham, I don't remember Anderson saying anything about that." The coach told his small squad that this game, right here, right now, was the crossroads of the season. Whichever path they chose would determine how successful they would be for the second half, not just of this game, but of the 1939 season.

Buzz Dean kicked off to Gradisnik to start the second half. The Badgers could not move the ball and Gage punted to Kinnick who made a short return to the Wisconsin 40-yard line. On the first play from scrimmage, Kinnick was hit hard by Gage—a stunning blow that made the Iowa halfback's head spin. Bill Green carried on second down for a two-yard gain over center. On third down, Kinnick dropped back and spotted Dick Evans open downfield and launched a long strike that "Whitey" grabbed on the Wisconsin eight and ran across the goal line for the touchdown. Kinnick's drop-kick missed, but Iowa had the lead 12-7.

The Badgers were not through yet, by any means. Gradisnik returned Buzz Dean's kick-off to the Wisconsin 23-yard line. He gained eight more over center on the first play from scrimmage, but was hurt and had to be replaced by Bill Schmitz.

Paskvan and Schmitz took turns running off-tackle and over center, with occasional end runs, to put together a drive of over seventy yards to the Iowa 9-yard line. Schmitz surprised the Hawkeye defense with a pass to Al Lorenz in the end zone for the second Badger touchdown. Gage attempted the extra point, but Evans blocked it and Wisconsin had to settle for a one point lead: 13-12.

Al Couppee received Gage's kick-off on the Iowa eighteen and made a sixteen yard return to the 34-yard line. After a short gain by Kinnick and an incomplete pass, the Hawks lined up to punt, but Kinnick faked the kick and Dean carried the ball to the Wisconsin 46-yard line and a first down.

The Hawkeyes were stymied by the stiff defense. The teams traded punts and pass interceptions before the quarter ended with the Badgers in possession of the ball at midfield.

Wisconsin wasted no time in opening up their offense. Schmitz tried a play-action pass, under a heavy rush, and the ball was intercepted by Buzz Dean. He managed to get to midfield before being tackled.

Kinnick wasted no time, either, in going to the air. A pass to Prasse and another to Couppee got the ball to the Wisconsin 29-yard line. The Hawks shifted to a short punt formation with Bill Green, probably the fastest man on either side, lining up in the left flanker position. Nobody could stay with him. Kinnick spotted Green open in the end zone and completed a perfect pass to him for the touchdown. Kinnick's good dropkick for the extra point put Iowa back on top 19-13.

Diehl, his knee seriously hurt, was replaced by Andruska.

The Badgers, with time running out, tried to mount drives and strike back from the air, but interceptions by Max Hawkins and Buzz Dean thwarted all attempts. Time was eaten up on runs by Green, Couppee, and Kinnick.

As the last minute approached, Anderson sent Ankeny in at quarterback for Couppee instructing him to "sit on the ball." The game ended Iowa 19-Wisconsin 13, and the Hawkeyes were back on the winning track.

Of the twenty-six men on the traveling squad, only about eighteen had seen action. Bergstrom, Hawkins, Tollefson, Enich, and Kinnick had played the entire sixty minutes. Of Bergstrom's first complete college game, Kinnick said, "He finished a college football course in one afternoon." They had come from behind twice on three touchdown passes from Kinnick. The *Chicago Tribune* carried a sub-heading: "It's Nile's Party."

*Charles "Chuck" Tollefson, guard
(courtesy: University of Iowa Archives)*

Roundy Coughlin, a Wisconsin sportswriter, said, "Never did I think that I would see the day when an 18-year old kid from Council Bluffs, Iowa [Al Couppee] out-quarterbacked the quarterback of the Four Horsemen [Harry Stuhldreher]." Al Couppee called the game the one " . . . that opened everybody's eyes." He recalled that one of the biggest thrills for him of the season happened after the Wisconsin game. On the way to the dressing room, Frank Carideo, who had been Couppee's boyhood hero, walked up behind the young quarterback, slapped him on the shoulder pad and said, "Hey, Al, you looked like Ol' Frank out there, you know that?" Couppee said years later, "I felt nine feet high."

The statistics were, not surprisingly, fairly even. The Badgers had 100 yards rushing to the Hawkeyes eighty-five. In the air, Wisconsin completed five of eighteen passes for 177 yards, while Kinnick was seven for fourteen and 126 yards. Wisconsin had fourteen first downs to Iowa's seven, but the Badgers had six passes intercepted.

Bill Diehl would not play again that season. His knee injury was too extensive. Bruno Andruska took over as the full-time center.

*BJ "Bruno" Andruska, center*
*(courtesy: University of Iowa Archives)*

X-rays of Jens Norgaard's neck showed a cracked vertebrae and Anderson would not permit the young end to risk more permanent injury—even the following season. Norgaard was fitted with a special steel and leather brace to wear when the pain increased. Years later, he still used the same brace on occasion. Norgaard was worried that news of his injury would adversely affect his chances for Air Corps flight training, so the extent of the injury was kept secret from friends and teammates. (A few years later, Major Jens Norgaard led a group of B-26 Marauders on an important bombing mission over Utah Beach during the Normandy invasion.)

The Hawks traveled back to Iowa City, emotionally drained but happy. Anderson, Carideo, and Harris begun making plans for the next game, their third road trip in a row, with Purdue.

# CHAPTER 8

## PURDUE: ON THE ROAD—AGAIN

The Boilermakers of Purdue had spent the entire week getting ready for the visiting Hawkeyes. The scouts had been following Iowa closely since the opening victory against South Dakota and were convinced that if they could shut down Kinnick's passing attack, they could defeat the Hawks in a duel on the ground.

Purdue had been selected as a favorite to win the Big Ten Conference title. They had a strong line, especially on defense, which had allowed just thirteen points against conference foes thus far. Their three great backs, known as "Three B's": Lou Brock, Mike Byelene, and Jack Brown, could run, pass, and kick with the best in the country. Brown was especially noted for his kicking ability and skill in pass defense. Once again, the Iowa team was the consensus underdog.

It was the third consecutive away game for the Hawkeyes. Other conference teams were still reluctant to schedule games in Iowa City for fear of low attendance and loss of gate receipt shares, as had been the case in the suspension days. Twenty-two thousand Homecoming fans filed into Ross-Ads Stadium for what they thought would be a scoring bonanza by both teams.

Eddie Anderson had made a few adjustments to the starting lineup. This time there was no "strategy" in who started as with the Wisconsin game. The healthiest players would start and stay in the game as long as they could.

Bill Diehl, of course, was gone and Bruno Andruska had worked hard to be ready at the center position. Ken Pettit and Ham Snider started at guards with Mike Enich and "veteran" Wally Bergstrom at the tackles. Erwin Prasse and Dick Evans started at the ends. The backfield would start with Kinnick, Murphy, McLain, and Couppee. Max Hawkins, Buzz Dean, and Bill Green were ready replacements, sure to see plenty of action.

The brisk wind was from the north and Brock, the Purdue captain, elected to kick with the wind advantage upon winning the coin toss. August Morningstar kicked off, but the ball went only fifteen yards where it was downed by the Iowa linemen.

Couppee called two successive reverse plays with Murphy carrying and the ball was advanced to Purdue territory. An end run by Kinnick to the right was good for nine yards, followed by a 7-yard gain by Murphy to the thirty and a first down.

Murphy made eleven yards on three successive runs over center with Andruska leading the way. On the third attempt, the play was called back due to an illegal motion penalty on the Hawks. On the next play, Kinnick went back to pass, but Brown intercepted the ball on his own 5-yard line and, behind great blocking, was able to return the interception to the Iowa 43-yard line.

The Boilermakers went to work with good field position. Brock ran twice off-tackle, moving the ball to the Iowa 34-yard line. On third down, DeWitte fumbled the ball and Al Couppee pounced on it for the Iowa recovery on his own 33-yard line.

Ed McLain tried his hand at the Purdue line, but made only a few yards on two tries. On third down, Kinnick launched a long pass to Prasse, but, once again, Brown snatched the ball away and was tackled at the Purdue 35-yard line.

A delay of game penalty against Purdue moved the ball back another five yards. Brock tried a run up the middle, but was stopped short by Bergstrom and Snider. On the next play, Brock surprised the Hawks with a quick-kick that rolled out of bounds on the Iowa 20-yard line.

Following an exchange of punts, the Hawkeyes found themselves with the ball on their own 21-yard line. Kinnick tried a long pass to McLain, but the ball was just inches beyond his reach. Kinnick gained nine yards around right end and Murphy plowed through the middle to the 32-yard line and a first down.

Another aerial attempt, from Kinnick to Murphy, was good for eleven yards. Kinnick's run around right end moved the ball to the Purdue 44-yard line through a wall of defenders. Runs by Murphy, McLain, and Couppee added eleven more yards. Kinnick was stopped for no gain as the first quarter ended.

Bill Green and Buzz Dean checked into the game, replacing Murphy and McLain.

The Hawks tried a reverse from Dean to Kinnick that was good for six yards. Bill Green smashed through the line for a first down on the Purdue 22-yard line. Runs by Dean, Green, and Prasse moved the ball to the eight. They were within striking range now, but the Boilermaker defense stiffened. Bill Green's drive up the middle made only two yards.

*Nile Kinnick #24 on a reverse play with Ray Murphy #69 lead blocking (courtesy:University of Iowa Archives)*

Al Couppee called the team into a rare huddle. He told them that the count on the next play would be on five, instead of the usual four. Hopefully, this would draw the defense offside, or at least surprise them. He told them, "We're going on five, so stay in there! Don't anybody jump offside!" Dean, the wingback, was sent in motion, took the ball, and ran out of bounds right at the goal line for an apparent touchdown.

But somebody had jumped too soon.

Couppee recalled, " . . . of all the guys, it was Kenny Pettit, the most conscientious, dedicated guy in the world." The play was called back. Couppee continued, "Kenny, to the day he died, never forgot the fact that he jumped offside and he would apologize to me every time he saw me no matter where we were . . . ."

Green tried over center again and made two tough yards. On the next play, Petry, the Purdue center, broke through and nailed Green for a loss of three yards. On fourth down, Kinnick tried a pass to Prasse in the end zone, but the throw was broken up by Byelene. The Boilermakers had held fast and took possession.

For the rest of the quarter, neither team could gain an advantage and play was pretty much limited to between the forties. Most of the plays were reverses, end runs, and an occasional pass. Wally Bergstrom recalled that on one tackle eligible pass play, "Kinnick made a perfect looping pass to me with no one between me and the goal line and I dropped the ball. The play was never called again."

The first half ended in a scoreless deadlock, but the fans had enjoyed a first-rate contest. The teams retired to their respective dressing rooms for the intermission.

Anderson was livid. The members of the backfield were sitting on a rolled up wrestling mat, catching their breath, when the furious head coach walked over, grabbed Al Couppee, and said, "Couppee, when we get down on the goal line, there's just one guy on this football team who should get that football! Do you even know who he is?! Why don't you meet Nile Kinnick!" He even wanted Couppee to shake Kinnick's hand. With Murphy and Green doing so well, the young quarterback had called their numbers time after time instead of Kinnick's. "I was embarrassed as hell," Couppee recalled.

The Hawks had moved the ball well on the ground, but could not cross the elusive goal line. It was a reminder of the Michigan game. At least the defense had held Purdue scoreless in return. It was clear that nobody could let up in the second half.

The third quarter was a repeat of the action in the later part of the second. The teams attempted a couple of running plays, and then punted. Each defensive line was like a brick wall. Each team had poor snaps from center on punt attempts, but neither caused a turnover and nobody could capitalize.

As the final quarter began, the Boilermakers had the ball deep in their own territory. Byelene was able to gain four yards off tackle, but was well short of the first down. Calvin lined up to punt the ball away, but Mike Enich charged through the line, and, along with Dick Evans, blocked the punt. Erwin Prasse recovered the loose ball and was tackled two yards short of the goal line.

Buzz Dean plunged over the line for half a yard and Kinnick dove just short of the goal. Kinnick tried again, but was thrown for a two-yard loss. On fourth down Kinnick carried the ball to the corner around end, but was run out of bounds inches short. Purdue took over.

Brown attempted a punt right away, but mishandled the snap and was tackled in the end zone for a two point safety for the Hawks. Iowa was on the board at last.

The Purdue kick-off (following the safety) went to Buzz Dean, who made a return of twenty yards to the Purdue 45-yard line. The Boilermakers would not yield and the Hawkeyes were forced to punt. Kinnick's punt sailed over the goal line.

Now it was Iowa's turn to stiffen. Great efforts by Evans forced Purdue to lose yardage and punt the ball away. Kinnick make a punt return of fifteen yards to the Purdue 45-yard line.

Three straight attempts by Bill Green left the ball two yards short of a first down. Kinnick's fourth down punt rolled out of bounds on the Boilermaker 10-yard line. Byelene, mixing running and passing plays, tried to spread the Hawkeye defense. But hard tackling by Couppee and alert pass defense by Green forced another Purdue punt. On the play, Mike Enich crashed through once again and blocked Brown's attempt. Wally Bergstrom and Brown raced for the ball which was bouncing around in the end zone. Both players dove for the pigskin. The officials ruled the recovery by Brown and the tackle was credited to Bergstrom for another Iowa safety. Bergstrom recalled, "I recovered the ball, but Brown soon got into the act and the referee awarded us two points instead of six."

Iowa 4-Purdue 0.

At that point, for all purposes, the game was over. Purdue kicked off to the Hawkeyes. Kinnick and Green, road-trip roommates, ate up the clock with over-center and off-tackle runs. The final gun sounded with the Hawkeyes threatening on the Purdue 30-yard line.

The Boilermakers had partially achieved their goal. They had shut off Kinnick's passing. The Cornbelt Comet had completed only one pass of eight attempts for a total of twelve yards. His four interceptions, by Jack Brown, prompted a newspaper subheading, "Kinnick to Brown—New Passing Combination."

The Hawkeye rushing attack more than made up for it. Kinnick had gained sixty-five yards; Green had forty-five; Murphy had forty-seven. Iowa runners accumulated 180 yards compared to Purdue's seventy-five yards of total offense. Eleven Iowa first downs to Purdue's four told the story on ball control.

Jim Harris, always ready with a clever remark, when asked about the score, said, "Shucks, we didn't even need that last safety. We just wanted to make it decisive."

Bergstrom, Andruska, Ken Pettit, Enich, Evans, Prasse, Couppee, and Kinnick had played the entire sixty minutes. Only three substitutes were used.

Mike Enich was declared the hero of the game by his teammates. Upon their return to Iowa City, a group of Hawkeye stars including Max Hawkins, Ham Snider, and Nile Kinnick told a waiting group of sportswriters, "If you guys don't give Mike credit for what he did today, you ought to be shot." The shy tackle would only smile in embarrassment.

Hundreds of students, university officials, and townspeople mobbed the team members as they got off the train at the Iowa City depot. There was even an impromptu parade as the players were pushed into waiting cars and driven around the city and campus with a band playing, along with the sound of car horns and cheering.

The realization began to sink in: they weren't just winners with a 3-1 record. They were legitimate contenders for the conference title. Illinois had beaten Michigan that day and Northwestern had beaten Minnesota. It made the Purdue victory even sweeter.

In a letter to his mother, Nile Kinnick said about the Purdue contest, "It was by far the best game an Iowa team has played as a whole since I have been down here. The line was magnificent."

The players, fellow students, and fans celebrated the victory with much noise and carrying on all week. Eddie Anderson, described by one sportswriter as "calm as a home-made swimming pool" was already planning for the next week. At last—a home game.

The opponent would be tough, well-coached, and undefeated-Notre Dame.

# CHAPTER 9

# NOTRE DAME: HOME AT LAST

During the week before the game with Notre Dame, Nile Kinnick wrote to his father, "Here is a ticket for you and three sideline passes for the lads. See you after the game .... Hold your hat." The young tailback knew what a big game it was going to be.

Game ticket for Iowa vs. Notre Dame, Nov. 11, 1939—
note the price of $2.75 (courtesy University of Iowa Archives)

In the history of college football, no team has obtained the tradition and wide-spread respect of Notre Dame. Even hardened foes must admit that no matter their won-loss record, the Fighting Irish are dangerous in every game they play.

Iowa had not played Notre Dame since Eddie Anderson had been the Irish captain and had been upset by the Hawkeyes in Iowa City. On this November Saturday in 1939, Notre Dame owned a six-game winning streak and was everyone's pick for the national championship.

Elmer Layden, Irish head coach and Four Horseman fullback for Knute Rockne, had a strong team, complete with size, speed, and depth. Harry Stevenson and Benny Sheridan shared the duties at left halfback: Stevenson was the better passer and punter, while Sheridan had blazing speed. Bernie Crimmons was the other halfback with Steve Sitko running the team at quarterback; Johnny Kelley was the Irish captain and played right end. Notre Dame was "blessed" with outstanding athletes playing behind other outstanding athletes at almost every position. Bob Saggau, Bud Kerr, and Lou Zontini were just a few of the other talented men whom Layden was counting on.

The previous week had been a busy one for Anderson and his staff. Much of the time was spent in perfecting the pass plays with Kinnick throwing to virtually every member of the team in practice. The players were pleased to welcome Henry Luebcke back to the practice field. Although he could no longer play, due to the injury and hernia surgery, he still enjoyed working out with his teammates and helping in any way possible.

Eddie Anderson would go with the same line-up as the previous week against Purdue. Andruska continued at center, improving every week, flanked by Ken Pettit and Ham Snider at the guards, with Enich and Bergstrom at the tackles. Prasse and Evans were the ends with the regular starting backfield of Kinnick, Couppee, McLain, and Murphy. Chuck Tollefson and Max Hawkins were ready when needed on the line with Bill Green and Buzz Dean prepared for backfield duty. Buzz Dean had jammed his shoulder the previous week and was fitted with a special brace like the one Al Couppee was wearing.

Over ten thousand well-wishers attended a pep rally at Old

Capitol on Friday night. Prasse and Enich represented the rest of their teammates who were safely sequestered in their usual hospital ward.

The next day, over forty-six thousand (some accounts put the number at over 50,000) fans arrived early on this crisp, sunny Saturday. Many had been to the big campus rally the night before. They had come to witness the outcome of the "rivalry" between Anderson and Layden, which had been built up all week by the media.

Notre Dame won the toss and elected to defend the south goal. Stevenson's kick-off sailed into the end zone and the Hawkeyes started from their own 20-yard line.

Kinnick opened up with a gain of twelve yards and a first down. But the Irish closed ranks and runs by McLain and Murphy could advance the ball only four yards. Kinnick's third down punt went to Sitko, who was tackled immediately on his own 25-yard line by Prasse and Couppee.

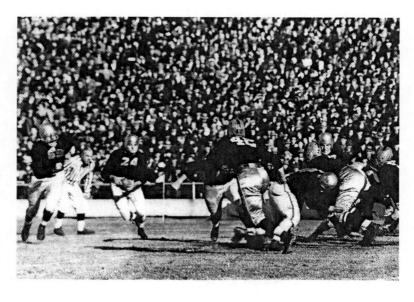

*Nile Kinnick #24 running behind blocking of Ray Murphy #69 and Erwin Prasse #37 (author's collection)*

A surprise quick-kick by Stevenson returned the ball to the Iowa 18-yard line.

Keeping the offense conservative, the Hawkeyes tried two running plays. An end run attempt by Kinnick lost two yards and McLain was able to gain only two through the line. Kinnick's punt from close to his own goal line went to Sitko near midfield. The return was good for nine yards and put the ball in Iowa territory.

Notre Dame decided to open up a little with Stevenson throwing passes to Crimmins, but the Iowa secondary thwarted the attempts. Crimmins tried an end run, but gained only a yard before he was stopped by Al Couppee. Crimmins was injured on the play and had to be replaced by Juzwick. Stevenson punted the ball to Iowa's 13-yard line.

The play continued; run two and punt for the Hawkeyes; pass, run, and punt for the Irish. The Iowa runners could not pierce the determined Notre Dame line. Couppee was reluctant to call pass plays against the wind, especially so close to his own goal line. Kinnick got off tremendous punts to keep the opposition out of striking range. Great tackles by the Iowa defense, especially by Andruska and Prasse, kept the South Benders from gaining first down yardage.

On the last play of the scoreless first quarter, Stevenson punted. It was a boomer. The ball sailed clear over Kinnick's head and he finally chased it down on his own 3-yard line where he was tackled by Kerr. The Hawks were deep in their own territory, but would have the wind advantage.

Elmer Layden substituted a completely new team to begin the second quarter. None of the Iowa starters had had a rest so far. Kinnick wasted no time in punting the ball away to gain some breathing room. Hargrove caught the ball at midfield, where he was smothered by Dick Evans.

Now against the wind, the Irish kept the ball on the ground. Bone crushing tackles by Prasse and Murphy denied the first down yardage.

Although they had the wind advantage, the tired Ironmen were facing fresh, rested opponents and could do little to gain yardage. It was back to the same run two plays and punt routine. All they seemed to be able to do was to stand tough on defense and watch for a break that would give them decent field position. Notre Dame was in the same boat. Time was being used up quickly with all of the running plays.

With the ball on their own 20-yard line following a punt, the Hawks were still in the shadow of their own goal post. Murphy scampered around left end and outdistanced the defense for a gain of fifteen yards. Couppee called a double-shift play to the right, but it gained nothing and McLain was injured. Buzz Dean replaced him. After a three-yard gain on a fake pass, Kinnick launched a rocket of a punt—fifty-two yards—to the Notre Dame 15-yard line, where Hargrove made the catch and a return of six yards.

Stevenson made eight yards off tackle. Piepul, on a reverse, made one. Stevenson, again through the Iowa line, broke free for eleven yards, almost shaking everyone loose for the touchdown, but Kinnick downed him on the 41-yard line.

With time running out in the first half, Stevenson fired a pass over the middle, but Kinnick intercepted the ball on the Iowa 45-yard line. Somehow, he managed to dodge six tacklers and return the ball to the Notre Dame 35-yard line.

Elmer Layden sent his first team back in.

Anderson sent in Bill Green to replace Murphy.

This was the break the Hawks had been waiting for. On the first play, Kinnick let fly a long pass to Buzz Dean in the end zone, but Sitko was there and grabbed the ball for the interception. He tried to return the ball upfield, but was hit hard by Andruska. The ball popped loose and Dean and Evans pounced on it. Iowa had the ball first and goal on the Notre Dame 4-yard line. This was it. They were not sure another chance would come.

Kinnick tried right end, but could make no headway. Buzz Dean met the same greeting off tackle. It was third down and Notre Dame called time out.

With the ball ready for play, Al Couppee called a rare Iowa

huddle. He remembered what Anderson had told him during halftime of the Purdue game (that Kinnick should be the ball carrier down close to the goal line). He also knew that the plays to the right had been shut off by the Notre Dame line.

Couppee told his teammates, "All right, we're going to run 31 Left (an off-tackle play) and I want Kinnick to go to right and Dean to go to left (halfback position)." A few of the senior players were against the idea, not wanting to make changes like this at the last minute, especially in such an important situation. But the sophomore quarterback insisted, "We're running that play the way I called it, let's go . . . ."

The ball was snapped directly to Kinnick. The Hawkeye line surged ahead. Kinnick was hit at the goal line, but he kept his feet and roared it through for the touchdown. His drop-kick for the extra point made the score 7-0 Hawks with forty seconds left in the half. The Irish could not advance the ball before the time ran out.

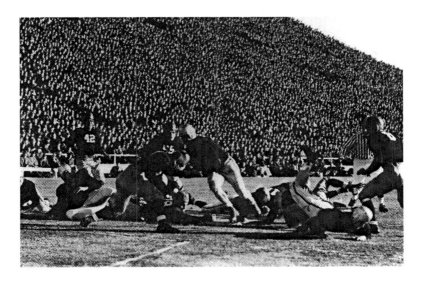

*Nile Kinnick's winning touchdown vs. Notre Dame*
*(courtesy: University of Iowa Archives)*

In the dressing room at halftime, Anderson asked, "Who was responsible for changing Kinnick to right halfback?" Everyone looked at Al Couppee, wondering what was coming next. Anderson said, "I want you fellas to know that's the smartest thing I ever had a quarterback do."

Couppee recalled, "That really took the heat off me."

Eddie Anderson addressed his team: "You men realize you're leading Notre Dame, unbeaten Notre Dame by seven points, and you've got thirty minutes of football to play. Every football team in the United States would like right now to be in your position. Thirty minutes left, and the greatest moment of your football lives is within your grasp. Now let's go out that door and finish the job!"

For the second half, Notre Dame had switched from their blue jerseys to green ones, possibly to create a better contrast to the black Iowa jerseys. Or it may have been to create some sort of psychological edge. In any case, the third quarter was a return to the run and punt action of the first half for both teams. For most of the third quarter, neither team could put a drive together.

Finally, starting from their own 25-yard line, the Irish started to wear down the Ironmen. Runs by Stevenson and Piepul were met by hard tackles on the part of Andruska, Green, & Co. Little by little, first down after first down, Notre Dame moved into Iowa territory. Ham Snider went down and was replaced by Chuck Tollefson. As the third quarter came to a close, the Irish had the ball on the Iowa 10-yard line.

Sitko opened the final period with a gain of four yards. On the next play Piepul punched through the line for a touchdown. The teams lined up for the critical extra point attempt. Zontini's place kick went wide to the left and the Hawkeyes retained a slim 7-6 lead.

The Hawks—truly Ironmen by this time—were tiring, but had the wind advantage. Elmer Layden kept substituting fresh players who continuously shut off the Iowa offense. But they could not shut off Kinnick's booming punts that kept the Irish backed up in their own territory.

Notre Dame kept the Hawkeyes with their backs to their own

goal, too. Even with the wind, plays were restricted to runs to avoid the dreaded interception and to use up time on the clock.

With two minutes left in the game and deep in his own territory, Kinnick had to punt once again. He knew it would be a critical kick and that Notre Dame would be rushing hard. He took the snap, spun the laces up, and booted it out.

Down at the other end of the field, Steve Sitko, awaiting the kick, looked up at the ball, unfastened his helmet and threw it on the ground in disgust. Kinnick's punt, possibly the longest of the year, flew far over the Notre Dame quarterback's head, hit the ground and bounced out of bounds on the 6-yard line. It was a sixty-one yard clutch kick—the final nail in the Notre Dame coffin.

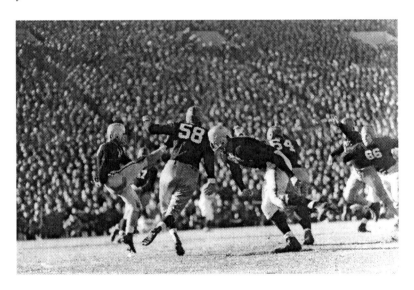

*Nile Kinnick's longest punt of the season, against Notre Dame (courtesy: University of Iowa Archives)*

Al Couppee recalled, "I turned around and looked at the scoreboard. It said 7-6 with two minutes left to play and I knew we had beaten Notre Dame. And I gotta tell you, that's the biggest thrill I ever had in football."

Of course, the Irish did not give up. But the Hawkeye defense was spread way out to guard against the big play. The linebackers were almost thirty yards off the line of scrimmage. On the last play of the game, Benny Sheridan, with most of his pads removed for extra speed, tried to break into the open. (The week before, Notre Dame had beaten Army on an identical play.) But Mike Enich chased Sheridan around and into the arms of Max Hawkins who tackled him.

It was all over. Little Iowa had upset mighty Notre Dame and the eyes of the nation were turned on this small band of Hawkeyes. Iowa had used only fifteen players—eight of them playing the full sixty minutes. Nile Kinnick, punting sixteen times, had played in his fifth consecutive sixty-minute game.

The Irish winning streak and championship dreams shattered. They had matched or exceeded the Hawkeyes in practically every statistical aspect of the game, except the most important one—total points.

Elmer Layden said, "I've remarked before that the Notre Dame football team is the greatest charitable institution anywhere, and it was proved again today." But he admitted, "But they played grand ball, it's no disgrace to lose a close one to a fine team like Iowa's." Irish ends Johnny Kelley and Budd Kerr went to the Iowa dressing room after the game and offered their congratulations to the courageous Hawks.

The fans stayed. They cheered. They celebrated. Monday classes were cancelled. A victory dance was organized at the Memorial Union. Some brought up the idea of a conference title, the first in years.

But the skeptics warned—What about Minnesota? The Hawkeyes never seemed to play well against the Golden Gophers-their arch rivals. They would have to wait a week for the answers to the questions.

# CHAPTER 10

## MINNESOTA: INVASION FROM THE NORTH

Much was at stake at Iowa Stadium on Saturday, November 18th—Homecoming, the Floyd of Rosedale Trophy, and possibly the Big Ten Conference championship. Each team had to win to keep its hopes alive.

*Nile Kinnick meets "Floyd of Rosedale" before the Minnesota game (courtesy: University of Iowa Archives)*

After a rare Monday off for a well-deserved rest, Anderson pushed the players the rest of the week, especially on technique concerning the passing attack. All team members participated in the throwing drills. On Thursday, Dr. Eddie closed the last part of the final practice session before the game to all except team members and the coaching staff. The buildup all week long had been incredible. News articles about the various team members and individual heroics appeared in the press. One writer dubbed Iowa's line as the "Seven Shells of Shrapnel." Of course, there were the usual "reports" of what the Minnesota players, officials, etc. had supposedly said about the upcoming game. Almost 6000 tickets were sold to Golden Gopher fans. On Friday evening, there was a large rally on the Old Capitol lawn featuring Anderson, members of the team, and some University officials. It was the type of atmosphere that can exist only before such encounters between college rivals.

*Eddie Anderson addresses pep rally crowd night before the Minnesota game (courtesy: University of Iowa Archives)*

Over 50,000 homecoming fans crammed into Iowa Stadium on Saturday. It was estimated that almost 10,000 school kids squeezed into the "knothole section" at the end of the field. Everyone was there to witness the "game of the decade."

Bernie Bierman, the top-rated Minnesota head coach, had also been preparing his team all week. Since taking over as head coach of his alma mater's football team in 1932, Bierman had won three national championships and four times won the Big Ten Conference (Western Conferenc) Championship. Unlike Anderson, who had been described as "calm as a homemade swimming pool," Bierman "showed the tension inside him the way he lit and discarded one cigarette after another on the sideline during a game." Each man had his own style—each one successful and each highly respected.

As always, the Gophers were big and tough. (Some Big Ten teams refused to play Minnesota. One season, Michigan had to play them twice to give the Gophers enough conference games.) Minnesota's interior line outweighed the Hawkeyes by an average of twenty-six pounds per man.

The backs were outstanding. Harold Van Every, at left half, was fast and an accurate passer. Bruce Smith, one of the right halfbacks, just a sophomore, was two years away from winning the Heisman Trophy, and already showing exceptional skills. George "Sonny" Franck, a Davenport, Iowa native, and future New York Giant, was also one of the stars, but was recovering from a knee injury. Excited to be playing close to home, he did not let on how serious the injury was.

"I wanted desperately to do well in that game," he recalled. "I really wanted to play and said that I was better than I was."

The tension was electrifying on both sides of the field as kick-off time neared. John O'Donnell, sports reporter for the Davenport newspaper, wanted to get a picture of Sonny Franck and Nile Kinnick together before the game. Both young men obliged. Franck remembers that after the picture was taken, "I said, 'Good luck, Nile,' but he never answered me . . . ." Kinnick and the rest of the Hawks were preparing for the game of their lives.

Anderson went with the same starting line-up as the previous week. Most of the players were healthy, except for the normal strains and bruises. Bruno Andruska had a bruised wrist, but not on the hand he used for centering the ball. Al Couppee and Buzz Dean were wearing their "horse collars."

Minnesota won the toss and elected to receive. Prasse's kick went to Mernick, a sophomore, who returned the ball from his own 10-yard line to the twenty-seven. Couppee delivered a blistering tackle and, in the process, injured his good shoulder, but stayed in the game.

After a gain of three yards off-tackle by Mernick, Van Every unloaded a long pass to Mariucci, who caught it and was tackled on the Iowa 32-yard line. Runs by Smith, Sweiger, and Van Every moved the ball to the twenty-seven. Then, on fourth down, Smith bolted around left end for a gain of twelve yards and a first down.

Van Every and Sweiger, keeping the ball on the ground, each gained two yards. On third down, the Gophers were guilty of holding and the ball was moved back to the 26-yard line. Smith's pass attempt to Memik was incomplete and Van Every's fourth down punt went beyond the goal stripe. The Hawks would have the ball on their own twenty.

Kinnick got the first call, but was dropped for a seven-yard loss by Mariucci. McLain's effort was for no gain and Iowa was penalized back to the one for holding. Kinnick punted the ball out to Van Every at midfield, who made a return of fourteen yards.

Van Every kept up the pressure with a gain of five yards over right tackle; Sweiger made two over center before being stopped by Couppee. Sweiger's three-yard plunge over center put the ball on the 23-yard line for a first down.

Two runs for no gain against the stiffening Hawkeye defense forced the Gophers to go to the air. The third down pass was incomplete and Mernick tried a field goal on fourth down, and missed. Iowa got the ball again on the twenty.

Kinnick's first down punt was a missile to the Minnesota 20-yard line, where Van Every received it and made a return of eleven yards. A Minnesota clipping penalty moved the ball back to the 31-yard line.

Mernick and Sweiger could not get the first down yardage and, with only a few seconds remaining in the quarter, Christiansen and Sonny Franck went into the game. Franck's punt was short and the Hawkeyes got the ball on their own 48-yard line-their best field position thus far. Murphy's spinner off right tackle was good for six yards and McLain made it two more on the other side. Murphy's run to the Minnesota 43-yard line made the first down. After a one-yard gain by McLain, Kinnick threw a long pass to Evans, but it fell incomplete. On the next attempt, Kinnick spotted Prasse downfield and let the ball fly, but Franck picked it off and returned the interception to his own 21-yard line.

Now the new running combination of Franck and Christiansen took over. With Christiansen blasting up the middle and Franck sweeping around the ends, the Gophers moved the ball to midfield as the scoreless first quarter ended.

Franck, Van Every, and Christiansen each had a turn at the Iowa line, but none could make more than a couple of yards, due to crushing tackles, mainly by Enich and Bergstrom. On fourth down, Van Every punted to Kinnick, who called for a fair catch on his own 11-yard line.

The Golden Gophers would not yield to the Hawkeye rushing attempts. Once again, Kinnick punted the ball away and it rolled out of bounds close to midfield.

Rushes by Franck and Van Every moved the ball to the Iowa 40-yard line and a first down. The tired Hawks called a time out. Al Couppee recalled the Minnesota squad as "one of Bernie Bierman's typical teams. They just beat you up something terrible."

Van Every ran for five yards and Franck made four more. Van Every slammed off right tackle to the Iowa 16-yard line. It looked like the weight difference was beginning to take its toll on the Hawkeye defense. But Ham Snider's two successive tackles—first on Van Every, then on Christiansen—put a hold on the Minnesota drive. Franck ran to the Iowa ten, but no further.

*Ankeny #11 and Andruska #14 try to block Minnesota kick (courtesy: University of Iowa Archives)*

Mernick's field goal attempt was good. Minnesota had scored first and led 3-0.

Paschka kicked off to Kinnick who received the ball in the end zone and managed a fifteen-yard return, but the Hawkeyes, staying on the ground, could not move the ball and Kinnick punted again. Franck returned the punt to midfield.

After a short gain and an incomplete pass attempt, Van Every tried a quick-opener, but fumbled the ball and Prasse recovered for Iowa on the Minnesota 42-yard line. Bill Green and Buzz Dean checked into the game.

Kinnick made a short gain, then, on second down, fired a pass to Evans, who caught the ball on the 30-yard line and made nine more yards before being hauled down by Van Every, Christiansen and Smith.

Buzz Dean's reverse attempt was good for a yard. Kinnick, under a heavy rush, launched a pass, but it was intercepted by Van Every with a "leaping, one-hand grab" on the 10-yard line. Time was running out and the Gophers were content to run Mernick and Van Every up the middle until the half expired.

The Hawks, although some were physically hurt, and down by three points, showed no signs of discouragement. They had held Minnesota to a single field goal, had proved they could move the ball against the Gopher defense, and would get the kick-off in the second half. The contest had just begun. If the Ironmen would ever have to live up to their name, the second half would be the time.

Minnesota's Pashka kicked off to start the third quarter. Kinnick, receiving the ball near his own goal line, made a return of twenty yards before being tackled by Sweiger and Pashka.

Bill Green's two rushing attempts moved the ball to within a yard of the first down. On third down, Buzz Dean crashed through the line for two yards, but the Gophers would not give up any additional first down yardage and Kinnick punted the ball out of bounds on the Minnesota 28-yard line.

Van Every and Sweiger tried bucking the Iowa line, but punishing tackles by Wally Bergstrom and Bruno Andruska made the runners pay for every inch. Mariucci hauled in a pass from Van Every and made it as far as the Iowa 33-yard line before being knocked out of bounds.

The Seven Shells of Shrapnel—plus four—stiffened to meet the threat. Van Every could make only two yards up the middle and Smith, on a left end run, was thrown for a loss of four yards. A pass attempt on third down fell incomplete and Van Every punted the ball to the Iowa 4-yard line.

As the Hawkeyes gathered to take their turn on offense, Bruno Andruska said quietly to a teammate, "I hurt my wrist." "Is it the wrist you hurt last week?" he was asked. "No, it's the other one," the young center replied. Andruska did not mention the injury again, but stayed in the game performing all of the duties at center. The wrist was broken.

Kinnick punted the ball right back to Van Every on the first play. The Minnesota halfback took the ball near mid-field and returned it to the Iowa 28-yard line.

Coach Bierman sent in some fresh players, including Sonny Franck, who made five yards on the first play by cutting inside his left end. Van Every made six more off tackle. Another run by Franck moved the ball to the twelve and Sweiger made a first down at the Iowa 7-yard line.

Sweiger and Franck hammered away at the Iowa line, but were stopped short both times by Mike Enich. Recalling the crunching tackles, Sonny Franck said, "he was the best player on the Iowa team." Van Every made only a yard. On fourth down, Franck took the ball from Christiansen and attempted a run around left end. He explained, "Van Every made a block on the end which allowed me to get outside, but the halfback forced me to the sideline and I drove into him. The ball was in the wrong arm, so when I hit the goal line, it was barely over the line."

The touchdown was a controversial one. Even though two officials were on top of the play, the Iowa fans booed their disbelief. Fifty years later, Al Couppee recalled, "I'm the guy that hit him and I know he was out of bounds." In any case, the touchdown counted. Mernick attempted the extra point, but the Hawkeyes blocked it. The score was now Minnesota 9-Iowa 0.

Mernick kicked off to Bill Gallagher, who was also playing hurt. His shoulder had been painfully sprained earlier. "Willie" took the ball on own 15-yard line and raced thirty yards before being stopped.

With the third quarter drawing quickly to a close, it was time for the Hawkeyes to open up the offense. Al Couppee was injured and out of the game, so Nile Kinnick was calling the plays. Kinnick's short pass to Prasse was incomplete as well as a long one to Buzz Dean. On third down, Kinnick tried another pass, this time to Bill Green, but Van Every intercepted the ball on his own 33-yard line.

Christiansen's two runs off tackle were good for a first down. A roughness penalty against the Hawkeyes moved the ball to the Iowa 40-yard line. Van Every tried an off-tackle plunge, but was tackled by Bruno Andruska for no gain and the third quarter ended.

Everybody was tired. Many were playing hurt. Besides Andruska and Gallagher, Ken Pettit's wrist was severely sprained. Buzz Dean and Chuck Tollefson were limping and Erwin Prasse's arm was badly bruised. Nile Kinnick's passing hand was swollen to nearly twice its normal size. Nobody complained. They knew they had to get something going quickly if they were to score enough points against these tough Gophers.

To open the final period, Bernie Bierman sent in Sweiger for Christiansen and Paffrath for Mernick. Van Every's dive up the middle gained only two yards. His punt sailed out of the end zone and the Hawkeyes were given possession on their own 20-yard line.

Kinnick knew he would have to throw the ball if Iowa was to have a chance of scoring at all against Minnesota—much less twice. But the swelling and numbness in his passing hand allowed him to throw only every other play in order to rest it on running plays.

The Hawks started with a short pass to Buzz Dean—good for ten yards and a first down. Kinnick gained eight yards around end and then passed again to Dean near midfield for another first down. Another Kinnick end run was good for two yards.

On the next play, Kinnick dropped back, looking for somebody open, and spotted Prasse heading for the goal. The Hawkeye captain caught the perfectly thrown pass on the 8-yard line and scampered into the end zone for a touchdown. Kinnick's drop-kick made the score Minnesota 9-Iowa 7. Suddenly the Hawks were back in the game.

Buzz Dean's kick-off went to Smith, who made an excellent return to the 32-yard line, where he slipped and fell. On first down, Smith ran through the left side for a gain of five yards. On second down, Sweiger was hit hard as he went through the line. The ball popped loose and Mike Enich recovered on the Minnesota 36-yard line.

Kinnick tried an end run, but was stopped for no gain. Bill Green swept around the other end and made eight yards before being dragged down by Pedersen. Kinnick's third-down pass to Prasse was incomplete.

*Kinnick #24 is stopped for a short gain up the middle against Minnesota (author's collection)*

There were ten minutes left to play.

On fourth down, Kinnick fired a pass, but it was picked off by Sweiger and Minnesota had the ball on its own 25-yard line. The Gophers, using Sweiger, Smith, and Van Every, kept the ball on the ground to use up time. But a five yard delay of game penalty, along with terrific tackles by Mike Enich, kept Minnesota from getting the necessary first down yardage.

On fourth down, Van Every kicked the ball away to Kinnick, who made a nine-yard return to his own 21-yard line. The Hawkeyes had only five minutes left.

Kinnick's pass attempt to Gallagher was incomplete. A pass, this time to Buzz Dean, was good for a first down on the 38-yard line.

On the next play, Kinnick, under a heavy rush, threw a pass that was intercepted by Van Every. The crowd groaned, but it turned to cheers when Minnesota was called for interference and the Hawkeyes retained the ball at midfield.

Harold Van Every recalled, " . . . I had intercepted the pass with about two minutes to go. Had we been given the ball we could have lasted out the two minutes and been the victor. However, there was an interference penalty called on one of our backs (I think it was Joe Mernick). Evidently one of the ends, that could have been Erwin Prasse, tripped as he jumped over Mernick who had fallen down. Interference was called and that gave Iowa back the ball . . . ."

Bill Green, on a left end run, moved the ball to the Minnesota 38-yard line. Gallagher was hurt on the play and Iowa called time out. Kinnick called his own number on a sweep around right end that gained ten yards before he was pushed out of bounds by Franck.

Once again, Kinnick dropped back to pass and spotted Bill Green in the end zone. Sonny Franck recalled the famous play: " . . . our guys gave Nile too much time to throw. I recall that Prasse and Evans ran a crossing pattern in front of me. As I tried to decide which one to cover, I looked for the ball and it was in the air going to Green. They really had three men open in the end zone." Green grabbed the ball for the touchdown. He was running so fast that he ran right into the temporary bleachers located in the south endzone. The crowd went crazy, surrounding the young back for several minutes before letting him return to the game. Kinnick's drop-kick for the extra point was blocked, but nobody seemed to care. The Hawks were out in front 13-9 with three minutes left to play in the game.

Vollenweider went in for Bill Gallagher.

Now it was the Gophers' turn to try to come from behind. Sonny Franck tried a long pass to Van Every, but it was broken up and nearly intercepted by Buzz Dean. Van Every's pass to Franck was incomplete and Bill Green stopped Van Every on the next play, short of the first down. Christiansen's plunge over center made the necessary first down yardage and Franck ran off tackle for five more. There was one minute left.

Van Every dropped back to pass, looked down field and launched a bomb, but it was intercepted at midfield by Nile

Kinnick. Two dives into the line by Kinnick used up the rest of the time. Final score: Iowa 13-Minnesota 9.

The Iowa fans mobbed the field and carried the players off on their shoulders. The Hawkeyes had clinched at least a second place conference finish. It was the first Iowa victory over their northern rivals in the last eight tries, and the Floyd of Rosedale trophy would remain in Iowa City this time.

Harold Van Every recalled, " . . . it was a tough loss for us. It was a very tough-nosed, hard-fought game right to the end."

Nile Kinnick had played his sixth consecutive sixty-minute game. Six other men, most with injuries, had also played the entire game: Prasse, Evans, Enich, Bergstrom, Ken Pettit, and Andruska.

Minnesota led in most of the statistics. The Gophers had 295 yards rushing to the Hawks 218 and sixteen first downs to Iowa's eight. And Minnesota had intercepted Kinnick four times. But Nile Kinnick had completed six important passes for 157 yards—with an injured hand—to put the winning points on the board.

Most of the Minnesota team members were too choked up to talk. Bernie Bierman (having his worst season at Minnesota) said, "I can't believe it. Those Iowa boys just can't be beaten and we can't win." However, he conceded, " . . . they have a scrapping ball club."

Bob Bjorcklund, the tough Gopher center, had to be helped down the steps to the dressing room. From the locker room, a frustrated Sonny Franck said, "That's the way it goes. It looks like we just aren't supposed to win. My knee was killing me, and that's an awful handicap on a fast man."

The joyous victory made the Ironmen's pain somewhat easier to bear, but there were some serious injuries. By Sunday, the list of injured included over half the starters. Al Couppee had severely sprained his shoulder and had a possible rib injury. Bruno Andruska's wrist had been x-rayed and confirmed to be a fracture. He was done for the season. He had, as Bert McGrane wrote, " . . . courage enough for a dozen men . . . ."

Ken Pettit's wrist was badly sprained, possibly broken, but he did not want it x-rayed for fear of missing the final game. Bill Gallagher had played with his shoulder badly sprained. Buzz Dean and Chuck Tollefson had leg injuries and Erwin Prasse's arm was bruised. It had been a costly victory.

To celebrate the win and reinstatement of Floyd of Rosedale, it was announced that there would be no roll call in classes on Monday. Al Couppee recalled that all that week, " . . . every time you'd walk across the campus—one of the players—the students would haul you up to Old Capitol and holler at you. They had spontaneous cheers and band maneuvers and every other thing. It was the darndest thing you ever saw in your life."

The victory is viewed as a classic, even today, decades later. But there was one more challenge to be met. And the injuries would make it difficult to get ready for the final game—at Northwestern.

# CHAPTER 11

## NORTHWESTERN: FINALE

It came down to the final game—another road trip. The Wildcats of Northwestern, coached by Pappy Waldorf, were not highly touted as contenders, but had proven their quality during the season. A win against Iowa would give them a share of second place in the conference. Their left halfback, Hahnenstein, was a triple-threat star like Kinnick, except faster. The Cats had plenty of healthy substitutes ready for the call. They would be ready for the Hawkeyes.

But could the Hawkeyes be ready? After the punishment taken in the Minnesota game, many of the Ironmen were nursing nagging injuries. Al Couppee, recalling that "... everybody was beat up ..." was wearing a brace on each shoulder and was a questionable starter. Sophomore George "Red" Frye would be starting his first Big Ten game at center in place of Bruno Andruska. A converted fullback, Frye was the last of the Iowa centers and knew that the Wildcat line would test him all day. Fifty years later he recalled, "Northwestern had an excellent team with outstanding guards, center and halfbacks. Hahnenstein—Method—Hayman-DeCorrevant. I realize I did at least a satisfactory job, but the important thing was that the coach could have called upon several of the other reserves and they could have done equally as well in their position. I think this indicates the whole squad was equally trained and conditioned to go all the way according to Dr. Eddie's philosophy: 'The team that's in the best condition will win.'" Most of the other young men would be able to start, but few were a hundred percent.

In order to share the conference championship, the Hawkeyes would have to beat Northwestern and hope that Michigan defeated unbeaten Ohio State. Before the game, Nile Kinnick received a telegram from Ed Frutig of Michigan, which roused the team. The Wolverine end said that if Iowa would take care of Northwestern, Michigan would take care of Ohio State.

*Kinnick and Anderson discuss pre-game strategy against Northwestern (author's collection)*

Over 40,000 fans were in Dyche Stadium on the late November day to view what they thought would be a high scoring contest.

Iowa won the toss and elected to kick with the wind. Prasse's kick was short and the ball was put in play by the Wildcats from their own 33-yard line. McGurn and Hahnenstein were unsuccessful in their rushing attempts, due to harsh tackles by Ray Murphy. Hahnenstein's punt was downed on the Iowa 33-yard line with no return. Kinnick handed off to Murphy on a reverse play, but he fumbled and the ball was recovered by Daly for Northwestern on the Iowa 42-yard line.

Runs by Chambers and McGurn and an incomplete pass by Hahnenstein left the Wildcats four yards short of a first down. Hahnenstein punted the ball away to the Iowa 17-yard line. Again, there was no return.

Most of the first quarter was much the same. Each defensive line was unyielding to the ballcarriers and neither team wanted to pass much so early in the game. The action took place mainly between the thirties as each team would "try two and punt." Two additional Iowa fumbles stopped drives before even getting started. Many of the Northwestern plays were run up the middle and the Wildcat defensive line did their worst to test the strength of Red Frye. But the young center held his own.

With time running out in the first period, Northwestern's Soper punted the ball out of bounds on the Iowa 43-yard line. Kinnick quick-kicked on first down and it was like a cannon shot—toward the Northwestern goal line where Bill Green downed it on the five.

Soper punted the ball from his own end zone out to near midfield. After short gains by Dean and Couppee, Bill Green found a big hole at right tackle and scooted through to the Northwestern 26-yard line. The next play was the same thing the other way with Green carrying to the 5-yard line.

There were some fresh purple jerseys as substitutions were made for the Wildcats to begin the second quarter. Green made a yard over left guard. His next attempt was off right tackle, but the ball was knocked loose and Chambers recovered for Northwestern on the three.

DeCorrevont punted the ball from deep in his own end zone. He was lucky to get the short kick away. Kinnick received the ball on the Northwestern 31-yard line and made a return of fourteen yards. The Hawks were threatening again.

With the fumble problems, it seemed like a good idea to go to the air, but passes to Evans, Prasse, and Dean were broken up by an alert Wildcat secondary. Northwestern took over on their twenty and elected to quick-kick. DeCorrevont really tagged the punt and the ball rolled out of bounds on the Iowa 37-yard line.

Three straight rushes by Bill Green left the Hawks just shy of first down yardage. Kinnick's fourth down punt went to DeCorrevont who went wide to his left from his own twenty and raced down the sideline to the goal. The crowd erupted in cheers, but their celebration was short-lived as the officials said that DeCorrevont had stepped out of bounds back on the 32-yard line.

On first down, DeCorrevont fired a pass, but the ball was intercepted by Buzz Dean near midfield. He made a ten-yard return, but fumbled as he was hit. Fortunately, Erwin Prasse recovered the ball at the 37-yard line.

Runs by Kinnick and Green advanced the ball five yards and a third down Kinnick pass slid off the fingertips of Bill Green. Kinnick's punt was downed by Mike Enich on the Wildcat 11-yard line.

DeCorrevont's return punt was a boomer that sailed way over Kinnick's head. When he finally got to the ball, at his 15-yard line, the Wildcat tacklers pounced on him. The punt had traveled 74 yards.

For a while, the two teams struggled again in the trenches. The kickers got a good workout as the teams exchanged punts twice more. The offenses were starting to open up a little now, mixing short passes with rushing attempts, and occasional fake passes. On one such play by Northwestern, Wally Bergstrom was injured and had to leave the game. Jim Walker, not yet fully recovered from the knee injury, went into the game at left tackle.

Hahnenstein launched a long third down pass to Smith, but Kinnick knocked it down. On fourth down, Hahnenstein got off another great punt that rolled out of bounds on the 1-yard line of the Hawkeyes.

Kinnick, from deep in his own end zone, kicked the ball away, but it was short and took a Northwestern bounce back to midfield.

Time was running out in the half as Ryan passed to Al Butherus, a reserve end, who made a great catch on the Iowa 8-yard line and was finally dragged down by Kinnick on the four. Hahnenstein ran twice over right tackle, getting the ball to the one. On third down, and with twenty seconds left in the half, Clawson went over right tackle and just edged into the end zone for a touchdown. Conteas' extra point kick made the score 7-0 and the crowd was ecstatic.

The kick-off went to Kinnick, who gathered it in on his 18-yard line and made an eighteen yard return as the half ended.

The Ironmen were still in the game, but the injuries were taking their toll. Bergstrom was out for good. Murphy was still in the game, but playing hurt, along with many of the others. Red Frye was badly beaten up with cuts and bruises, but was handling the job at center and linebacker. Dean and Couppee's shoulders were holding up, but nobody knew for how long.

Buzz Dean kicked off to start the second half. The return by Chambers was for twenty-eight yards to his own 33-yard line. His first down run over left tackle was good for thirteen yards before Kinnick ran him out of bounds. Hahnenstein got a turn and found a large hole off right tackle and he gained eight yards.

On second down, Hahnenstein's pass was intercepted by Red Frye who made an eight yard return to midfield. The Hawks took to the air with Kinnick flinging passes to Prasse, Dean, and Green, but the Wildcat defense was unrelenting and even the short completions weren't enough for first down yardage. Twice Kinnick was sacked hard behind the line.

Following a Kinnick punt, Northwestern put the ball in play on the 38-yard line. Keeping the ball on the ground, Hahnenstein and McGurn—alternating the rushing chores—started gaining seven and eight yards at a crack until the ball was inside the Hawkeye 30-yard line. Iowa called time out.

The final score of the Michigan-Ohio State game was hung on the scoreboard. The crowd cheered as they learned that the Wolverines had upheld their end of the bargain by upsetting the Buckeyes 21-14.

Hahnenstein, Chambers, and McGurn were now taking turns at the exhausted line of Ironmen. McGurn was forced out of bounds by Kinnick at the 19-yard line for a first down. During the tackle, the Iowa hero severely injured his shoulder, but said nothing and stayed in the game.

With their backs to the wall, the Hawkeye defensemen stiffened. Hahnenstein tried twice, but was cut down by Prasse and Enich. Chambers had a turn over right guard, but got only three yards. On fourth down, Hahnenstein gave it his best effort, but was stopped cold by Jim Walker.

Kinnick's first down punt was downed on the Northwestern 42-yard line and the Ironmen prepared for another Wildcat attack. After a short gain by McGurn over right guard, Evans hit McGurn on his second down attempt. On the next play, Hahnenstein dropped the ball and Evans pounced on it at midfield for the Hawks.

A first-down pass from Kinnick to Evans was good to the Northwestern 31-yard line, but Nile's shoulder was causing him so much pain Buzz Dean had to take over the passing duties. Two pass attempts by Dean were broken up. On third down, Dean went back to throw, but could not find anyone open and was sacked by Cutlich and Grefe for a loss of eleven yards. Ham Snider was injured on the play, but stayed in the game. But Nile Kinnick, his shoulder useless, and in much pain, could go no further. The courageous young halfback left the game and was replaced by Murphy. It would be discovered later that Kinnick had separated his shoulder on the earlier tackle. Number 24 had played his last game for the Old Gold.

Buzz Dean, now doing the punting, kicked the ball out of bounds on the Northwestern 11-yard line. Once again, the Wildcats put their running attack in gear. Hahnenstein and McGurn plugged away at the sagging Hawkeye defense. On a second down run up the middle, McCurn fumbled and Mike Enich recovered for the Hawks on the Northwestern 22-yard line.

Ray Murphy ran twice and moved the ball to the eleven. Chuck Tollefson was hurt and replaced by Max Hawkins. Green was thrown for a three-yard loss on a left end sweep. Murphy got the three yards back over left tackle. Russ Busk replaced Bill Green as the third quarter ended.

Al Couppee grabbed a short pass from Dean and was stopped immediately on the six. Dean's pass to Prasse was incomplete, but McGurn was called for pass interference on Prasse and the Hawks got the ball on the one—first and goal to go. They could not afford to let this break slip away. Murphy tried diving over center, but was stopped short. On the next play, Murphy, behind fierce blocking by Max Hawkins and Jim Walker, blasted through left tackle on a spinner and scored the touchdown. The Iowa fans finally had something to cheer about.

Buzz Dean, who had never place-kicked in a game before, made a perfect kick for the extra point, tying the game at seven. They had come back, exhausted and hurt, without their star halfback.

McGurn took Dean's kick-off on his own 17-yard line and made a return of thirty yards to near midfield. It was beginning to get dark now, and the Wildcats knew they needed a good sustained scoring drive to use up time.

With DeCorrevont and McGurn doing most of the work, and with the help of an Iowa penalty, the Wildcats marched down the field to the Iowa 5-yard line where the Hawks called a time out. Green came back into the game for Busk.

Time after time the Northwestern backs tried to dive over or crash through the solid Iowa defense. On fourth down and inches, Clawson leaped high in the air, but was met and stopped by Mike Enich. It was as close as the Wildcats would get for the rest of the game.

Dean punted the ball away. Northwestern tried to put together another drive, but alert defensive efforts, especially by Hawkins and Enich, kept the Wildcat runners in the hole.

The strain was beginning to tell on the Ironmen. Couppee was hurt, but in the game. Ray Murphy was taken out and was being kept on the sideline under observation. He was replaced by Henry Vollenweider. There were but a few minutes left in the game when the Hawkeyes got the ball on their own 20-yard line following a missed Northwestern field goal. The Hawkeye lineup was now made up of exhausted, hurt players, some playing unfamiliar positions. Al Couppee was calling pass plays to move the ball down the field quickly. Ed McLain was at tailback now and Couppee recalled, " . . . Ed couldn't throw the ball very good—no better than I could. It was just a conglomeration of a gutty bunch of guys sticking it out to the bloody end."

McLain did complete a pass to Green who made a first down on his own 35-yard line. Runs by Vollenweider and Green gained five more. On an end around play, Prasse was cut off and attempted a hurried pass that fell incomplete. Darkness was really setting in now. It was difficult to identify jersey numbers from more than a few yards away.

With a minute left to play, Anderson, under the mistaken assumption that a tie would be as good as a win, and disturbed by all the passing plays, sent Ankeny in for Couppee with instructions to "sit" on the ball. As Couppee came off the field, Anderson grabbed and shook him and said, "Are you all right, Al? Are you all right?" Dr. Eddie thought his young quarterback had "gone goofy" calling the dangerous pass plays. Couppee acknowledged that he was O.K., but Anderson did not believe it and kept him on the sideline.

On fourth down, McLain punted the ball to the Northwestern 28-yard line. A fake pass by Soper moved the ball to midfield. But the Hawkeye pass defense was alert and foiled an attempt to Smith. Soper went back to try one last pass, but was tackled on the 46-yard line as the game ended. Iowa 7-Northwestern 7.

It was a bitter pill to swallow. The courageous little group from Iowa City had been stopped just short of their dream. However, it was incredible that they did as well as they did against the 'Cats, considering their physical condition. It is doubtful, with such a makeshift offense, that they would have scored at the end-even with more pass plays. Anderson later apologized to Couppee for taking him out of the game and admitted his error.

The game was now history. Northwestern had dominated offensively, with twice as many yards rushing and passing (214 to 106). The game saw over thirty punts and eleven fumbles (seven by Iowa). But the Hawks had persevered on defense and it is a tribute to those men that they could stop so many Northwestern drives. Ohio State was the undisputed winner of the Big Ten for 1939, with Iowa second. Purdue took third and Michigan and Northwestern tied for fourth place.

Eddie Anderson treated his worn out warriors to a night in Chicago, putting them up at the Loop's Morrison Hotel and suspending all training rules and curfew. The next day they attended the Bears/Cardinals pro football game at Wrigley Field before heading home to Iowa City. The 1939 season was officially over.

*"The Survivors" of the 1939 season taken before Northwestern game (courtesy: University of Iowa Archives)*

*Front row, left to right:*
James J. Walker; Floyd R. Dean; Russell H. Busk; Jack V. Edling; Kenneth J. Pettit

*Second row, left to right:*
Herman Snider; Nile Kinnick; Erwin Prasse; Mike Enich; Richard Evans; William Gallagher; Jens Norgaard

*Third row, left to right:*
Joseph L. Moore; Robert J. Otto; Carl C. Conrad; Matt S. Miletich; Burdell Gilleard; Henry L. Vollenweider; Max S. Hawkins; Coach Eddie Anderson

*Fourth row, left to right:*
Charles W. Tollefson; William C. Green; James R. "Ray" Murphy; George D. "Red" Frye; William F. Diehl; Wallace Bergstrom; Gerald Ankeny; Albert Couppee

# CHAPTER 12

## AFTERMATH

And so they finished second. But the Ironmen were first in the hearts and minds of their fans, who greeted their return to the campus with the fanfare and celebration usually reserved for national heroes.

In a way, they were. The exploits of this small group of young men had captured the affection and admiration of football fans across the Midwest—a respect and awe that remains today. Across the heartland, in countless schoolyards and sandlots for years to come, young boys relived that 1939 season, taking turns "being" the triple-threat Kinnick, the fleet-footed Prasse, the cocky field general Couppee, and other members of the squad.

The University Athletics Department was pleased for another reason. The football season had generated over $85,000 of revenue. Small change compared to today's massive budgets, but a lot better than the $10,000 loss the previous year. Eddie Anderson and his assistant coaches were all given raises.

The post-season honors, both individual and collective, were many. Erwin Prasse, Mike Enich, and Nile Kinnick were named to various All-America teams. Kinnick, Buzz Dean, Erwin Prasse, and Dick Evans were selected to play on the *Chicago Tribune* All-Star team, who played the Green Bay Packers in Chicago in August of 1940. (Prasse was unable to participate due to a baseball commitment.)

Eddie Anderson was selected as head coach of the All-Stars, who made a good showing against the pros despite being defeated 45-28. Nile Kinnick, who had received the highest number of votes, directed the first scoring drive and drop-kicked the extra point that established the Stars' only lead of the game.

For his remarkable performance during the 1939 regular season (among other things, playing 402 out of a possible 420 minutes and scoring 107 out of the 135 Hawkeye points), Kinnick received a multitude of honors. Besides getting over a million votes for the All-Star team, Nile edged out such great athletes as Joe DiMaggio and Joe Louis to win the Outstanding Male Athlete Award for 1939. He also won the Maxwell and Walter Camp trophies and was the first unanimous winner of the Chicago Silver Football Award which is given to the Big Ten Conference's most valuable player.

Of course, he also won college football's most coveted award: The Heisman Trophy. His acceptance speech, given in New York at the Downtown Athletic Club (without notes) is considered a classic and is even more impressive when heard as well as read:

> *Thank you very, very kindly, Mr. Holcomb. It seems to me that everyone is letting their superlatives run away with them this evening. Nonetheless, I want you to know that I'm mighty, mighty happy to accept this trophy this evening. Every football player in these United States dreams about winning that trophy, and of this fine trip to New York. Every player considers that trophy the acme in recognition of this kind. The fact that I am actually receiving this trophy tonight almost overwhelms me. And I know that all those boys who have gone before me must have felt somewhat the same way. From my own personal viewpoint, I consider my winning this award as, indirectly, a great tribute to the new coaching staff at the University of Iowa headed by Dr. Eddie Anderson [APPLAUSE] and to my teammates sitting back in Iowa City. [APPLAUSE] A*

*finer man and a better coach never hit these United States, and a finer bunch of boys and a more courageous bunch of boys never graced the gridirons of the Midwest than that Iowa team of 1939. [APPLAUSE]—*

*I wish that they might all be with me tonight to receive this trophy. They certainly deserve it. I want to take this grand opportunity to thank, collectedly, all the sports writers and all the sportscasters and all those who have seen fit, have seen their way clear to cast a ballot in my favor for this trophy. And I also want to take this opportunity to thank Mr. Prince and his committee, the Heisman Award Committee, and all those connected with the Downtown Athletic Club for this trophy and the fine time that they're showing me, and not only for that, but for making this fine and worthy trophy available to the football players of this country. Finally, if you will permit me, I'd like to make a comment which in my mind is indicative perhaps of the greater significance of football and sports emphasis in general in this country and that is, I thank God I was born on the gridirons of the Midwest and not on the battlefields of Europe. [APPLAUSE]*

*I can speak confidently and positively that the players of this country would much more, much rather struggle and fight to win the Heisman Award than the Croix de Guerre.*

*Thank you. [APPLAUSE]*

Some of the honors came later. Mike Enich was elected to captain the 1940 Hawkeye team, and Bill Diehl was elected the following year to lead the '41 Hawks. Prasse, Enich, Diehl, and Kinnick were later named to the University of Iowa "All Time Player Squad" with Kinnick named as Best Football Athlete. Wally Bergstrom was named to the all-time list of Finest Single Season Performers in Football, for those who, for various reasons, only competed for one year.

In 1951, Erwin Prasse was selected as Iowa's best All-Around Athlete in the school's history for his 9 letters (football, basketball, and baseball). Also in that year, Nile Kinnick was elected to the College Football Hall of Fame. Eddie Anderson and Frank Carideo were elected to the Hall some years later, due primarily to their exploits at Notre Dame.

Legends have formed down through the years about the Ironmen. People debate about why the Hawkeyes were able to put together such a successful season after so many years of disappointment. Most of the credit, of course, goes to Nile Kinnick, whom Al Couppee describes as "the greatest single force on the field." Most of the team members contacted for this research believe much of the credit should go to Coach Eddie Anderson, who was named Coach of the Year for 1939. He was responsible for the discipline, the organization, and the motivation.

Max Hawkins, from his home in the shadow of Kinnick Stadium in Iowa City said, "We were a team of high achievers." Al Couppee agreed, pointing out that it took a lot of mental, as well as physical aptitude to learn and perfect the complicated Anderson system. He recalled only twice during the entire season that serious mental errors were made.

The physical conditioning, offensive system, and motivation can certainly be traced to Anderson and his staff. But the team members themselves—the actual 60-minute men, the regular players, and the other important squad members—should be given credit for their commitment to the program, and each other.

Eddie Anderson, in later years, took every opportunity to praise the team work of those squad members who, though they didn't play very much, were a vital part of the team's success. He said any success realized by the regular players was largely due to those who practiced hard, without complaint, often scrimmaging against the first team during the week, representing the upcoming opposition (called the "scout team"). Players like Carl Conrad, Matthew Miletich, Ambrose Callahan, Robert Herman, Robert Leighton, Carl Vergamini, Stephen Swisher, Phil Strom, Jack Edling, John Maher, and Warren Junge played very little, if at all, following the South Dakota game at the start of the '39 season. But their hard work on the practice field each afternoon helped the starters prepare. That, as Eddie Anderson reminded anyone who would listen, takes a special kind of selfless dedication.

That dedication to excellence would stand them in good stead the rest of their lives. Almost all of them went on to achieve great things in the uncertain war-torn and post-war world.

Some, like Al Couppee, Dick Evans, and Chuck Tollefson, went on to play professional football—Couppee with the Washington Redskins and Evans and Tollefson with the Green Bay Packers. Erwin Prasse played briefly on both professional baseball and basketball teams. Others, like Jim Walker, Phil Strom, Robert Otto, Matthew Miletich, George Falk, and Carl Vergamini went into education and became successful coaches and teachers at the high school and college levels.

The achievements were not limited to the world of sports. Many became leaders in their respective business communities. Wally Bergstrom, Ray Murphy, and Erwin Prasse became skilled in the insurance business. Henry Luebcke and Ed McLain were part of the Chicago business world. Red Frye retired as a hospital administrator.

Some of the men stayed in Iowa following graduation. Max Hawkins became a highly-respected resident of Iowa City, spending much of his life in the real estate profession and, for a time, as a respected legislative activist for the University. He even had an Iowa City street, Hawkins Drive near the stadium, named after him. Ham Snider helped run his family's successful Iowa City food business until his death. Bill Diehl, Bill Green, and Jerry Ankeny worked for Iowa-based manufacturing firms.

Most of the Ironmen were in the thick of the fighting during World War II, some of them, like Erwin Prasse, Mike Enich, Ken Pettit, overcoming serious wounds. Enich and Pettit returned to Iowa Law School and went on to have distinguished careers in the Iowa courts with Enich eventually becoming an Iowa District Court Judge.

Two of the team members did not survive the war. One was Burdell "Oops" Gilleard, an orphan, who was drafted into the army during his junior year and killed in action in New Guinea toward the end of the war. His Iowa teammates helped coordinate the return of his body to be buried in the National Cemetery at Keokuk, Iowa.

Some, like Bruno Andruska, (Colonel Andruska) and Buzz Dean, made the military a career. Jens Norgaard, his injured vertebrae a safe secret, served as a pilot instructor (as did Bill Green) and squadron commander. He flew the lead plane for the 9th Air Force support mission for the Normandy invasion. After serving in France and Belgium, he left the service as a Lt. Colonel and began a distinguished career as an engineer for Standard Oil of Indiana.

It is safe to say that there will never be another team like the Ironmen of Iowa. To be sure, there will be, and have been, other great Iowa football teams, playing more games a season in front of bigger crowds. (Today they do it in "Kinnick Stadium" so renamed in the 1970s). Other players will win prestigious awards and other honors. Forest Evashevski and Hayden Frye have fielded great teams with better records and outstanding statistics. Future Hawkeye head coaches will do the same.

But they would probably agree that it would be quite an impossible task to surpass what the little band of unranked Hawkeyes did in 1939. The records will fall and the athletic skills will continue to improve. But when the comparisons are made of great teams, the Ironmen will remain the unreachable model to all.

What they did in one short, eight-game season in a more innocent time in history, stands as a testimony to the importance of hard work, commitment, mental fortitude, and teamwork—not just in sports, but in all of life.

Their achievements and perseverance continue to influence those who saw them play in 1939, and those who listen to the stories for decades to come. The legend will continue.

## CHAPTER 13

## NILE KINICK:
## THE QUIET LEADER

The sea was calm and the sky a brilliant blue in the Gulf of Paria off Trinidad on the June morning in 1943. The aircraft carrier Lexington was conducting training maneuvers with a small escort force. The exercises included the normal launching and recovery of fighter and torpedo aircraft.

At about 9:30 a.m., one of the airborne planes—a Navy Grumman F4F-4 Wildcat single-seat fighter—developed a serious oil leak. The pilot, a navy ensign, called the ship to report an emergency. According to Bob Considine's column later that week, the pilot was calm and businesslike in his handling of the situation. But he knew the Wildcat's engine could not last long and was aware of the trickiness of a forced landing with no power on water. He also knew that the Lexington's deck was crowded with other aircraft waiting to take off and an immediate landing on the carrier would endanger many lives.

LEXINGTON: "Can you give us ten minutes?"

PILOT: "I'm not sure, but I'll try."

But the engine would not give him the time he needed and the pilot was forced to attempt a water landing.

The Grumman Wildcat was notorious for sinking quickly in a "ditch" situation. It was also known for having seat belts that would let go under sudden impact.

F4F-4 Number 7 made a perfect textbook landing in calm seas at Latitude 10°28' North, Longitude 62°15' West, about four miles in front of the carrier. Rescuers were on the spot in a matter of minutes, but all they found was empty ocean. No trace of Ensign Nile C. Kinnick was ever found.

The young man who had been an inspiration to teammates and opponents alike, who had so often turned defeat into victory, was suddenly gone at the age of twenty-four.

The sporting world and people in the midwest were shocked. Certainly this sensitive, intelligent future leader could not be gone. They waited for news that somehow it was all a mistake and that Nile had come through after all, as he had so many times on the gridiron.

Bill Green's words summed up what everyone was thinking: "Back in '39 when the going was tough in that last quarter, somehow I always felt Nile could throw one of those passes, even up to the last minute, and save the game."

But for Nile Kinnick, the game was over. "I doubt if he ever lost, except when time ran out on him," recalled Sonny Franck.

*US Navy Ensign Nile C. Kinnick*
*(courtesy: University of Iowa Archives)*

Lt. Commander Paul Buie of Nile's squadron, in letters to Mr. and Mrs. Kinnick, said, "Nile was making a wide arc of the carrier to avoid interference with the launching of a second group of planes he spotted on the flight deck." About the crash, he said, "The best guess . . . is that his safety belt broke on landing allowing Nile to lurch forward upon impact, probably striking his head on the structure of the airplane and injuring him to the extent that he could neither maintain himself afloat nor remember to inflate his life jacket."

Nile had given up a Rhoades Scholarship to attend Iowa's law school. But after a year, during which time he helped coach the freshmen and scouted for Anderson, he realized war was imminent and enlisted in the Naval Air Service. His diaries and letters, preserved by his father and donated to the University of Iowa Library, depict a truly sensitive and mature young man, certainly destined for greatness in politics or law. His insight and common sense, coupled with a drive to do his best at all times, are rarely found in such a young person. He enjoyed new challenges and tried to excel in every one.

Sometimes his innocence resulted in humorous situations. Al Couppee recalled one incident: "On one of our football trips in 1939, the Iowa team stayed at the Morrison Hotel in Chicago; fullback Ray Murphy and I (then only 18 years old as compared to Kinnick at 21) were walking down the hall toward the elevator. Nile stepped out of his room and joined us. As we approached the elevator, a hotel maid, a jolly-looking fat gal, stepped out of a room, and Kinnick said to her, 'Pardon me, do you have the time?' The maid giggled and replied, 'Yeah, but I ain't got the inclination.' Murphy and I broke up laughing, but Kinnick was mildly offended and had to ask us in the elevator what was so funny."

But there was nothing naive about Nile's feeling of duty and honesty. About his enlistment and future military service he wrote, "May God give me the courage to do my duty and not falter. This isn't a dramatic speech . . . it is honestly the way I feel."

To a friend and fellow classmate, Loren Hickerson, Nile wrote, "Let us hope that you and I, and many, many others like us will be enabled, someday, somewhere, somehow to contribute in some small way to the peace and progress of this world."

It is unlikely that Nile would have liked the cynical, paranoid postwar world and the nuclear age. Simplicity and innocence were gone forever, giving way to suspicion and fear. But it is even more unlikely that he would have allowed himself to be deterred from rolling up his sleeves and giving of himself, whether in the courtroom, political arena, or even as a flour salesman (which he once claimed he would enjoy being) to do his best for mankind. Responsible, sensitive people cannot help but give the full measure even when in the minority. But he was compelled to give the fullest of measures, as many good young men did, too soon, and it is the modern world's loss.

But his example still lives—influencing those born long after his gridiron exploits. Max Hawkins said, "He set the pattern of hard work on the practice field as he was always striving for perfection."

Al Couppee, speaking of Nile's leadership, remarked, "Nile never led, ever, by talking. It was what he did out there. He led by example. He was just—Kinnick, an indescribable human being."

Such an example of leadership and sensitivity like Nile Kinnick's never dies.

> *A man must never cease growing,*
> *developing, looking ahead. Be alert, be*
> *vigorous, cultivate the mind and memory*
> *continually—laugh a lot.*

> Nile Kinnick (May 6, 1943)

# CHAPTER 14

## LETTERS

*1939 Team Members:*

**29 September, 1985**

Dear Scott,

    How about a pencil-written message on a tablet? I was glad to hear from you. I remember your great uncles and their heroics as growing up on a farm 40 miles south of Iowa City. I saw them play when I was a knot-holer. Now *there's* a prime example of inflation: 25 cents to 15 dollars! I was a big Iowa U. football fan all my life. I wish I could provide you with some interesting material concerning me that you wouldn't already have, but as you know, linemen don't usually make much news.

    I had never played football competitively though I had been out as a freshman and a few days before school started in 1936. Then I didn't do anything more in regard to football until the Spring of 1939 after I had been in South America working on a coffee boat.

    Two of my regrets of the season were that I had 2 chances to score a touchdown but didn't. One is the tackle of Brown for a safety. When Enich blocked the punt I recovered the ball, but Brown soon got into the act and the referee awarded us 2 points instead of six. The other was a tackle eligible play. Kinnick made a perfect looping pass to me with no one between me and the goal and I dropped the ball. The play was never called again.

Sorry I couldn't provide more. Good luck.

Sincerely,

Wally Bergstrom

## 5 February 1985

Dear Friend Scott,

I knew of the Fisher brothers, Darrell and Ray, and of Russ, and I always had great respect for them as football players. They were at Iowa during an extremely difficult time for athletes. Much of what has been written about the Ironmen and Kinnick in the later years has been created out of rumor or simply lack of information. You are to be commended for at least going to the horse's mouth for your research.

As for Kinnick, it's a consensus among his onetime teammates that, had he lived a normal lifetime, he would have become our President, the Chief Justice of the Supreme Court, or something equally as mind-boggling. Nile was a totally unique human being, the most self-disciplined young person I've ever known, and at the same time a warm and outgoing guy. He exploited every opportunity tossed his way to learn, to improve himself physically, mentally, and morally, and at the same time Nile was naive and innocent of many worldly things.

He was a great, natural athlete but small (5'8" and 170 pounds at most) and he was NOT fast. He was an outstanding basketball player, All-Big Ten selection as a sophomore, but he quit basketball because it interfered with his idea of what he should be doing academically. He was also a marvelous baseball catcher, at one time in American Legion baseball Bob Feller's batterymate, but gave that up also in favor of football and academics. He simply liked to play the game of football, and that, along with his education, occupied his time at Iowa.

He was a practicing Christian Scientist. After making All-Big Ten as a sophomore halfback in 1937, Nile suffered an ankle injury early in the 1938 season. I was a freshman footballer then and scrimmaged against the varsity regularly. I saw Kinnick try to do things on that ankle, and the pain just wouldn't allow proper functioning of the ankle. Yet, he refused all medical aid and suffered through the entire season only a shadow of the player he had been and would be the following year. Nobody really knows if the ankle was broken, but my guess would have been that a bone or bones in the ankle had been broken and healed by themselves in the course of time. I admired his personal discipline and physical toughness, but I thought he was nuts not to have gone in for medical treatment.

Kinnick was not a leader in the sense of rah-rah or vocally directing or bossing. I don't remember one single instance the entire 1939 season when Nile said anything to me in the nature of advice or encouragement or critically. He just didn't talk, he performed. Kinnick led by example, on the practice field and in the games. Surpisingly, Nile Kinnick was the slowest and smallest of the backs who played most of the games in 1939. I think everybody but me could outrun Nile. He was shorter and lighter than any of the other five guys who managed the backfield positions during most of our games.

Something few people knew—Kinnick was awfully close to being ambidextrous, both foot and hand. He did, once, throw a running pass left-handed, but I don't recall which game it was. Kinnick did work occasionally in practice on throwing lefthanded, and even semi-seriously did some punting and drop-kicking leftfooted. So far as I know, Kinnick was the last man ever to actually DROPKICK points in a major college football game.

As for the 1939 Iowa football team and its incredible legend, I can only point to the motivation provided by Dr. Anderson, the leadership of Coach Eddie and his assistants, the example provided by Kinnick, the chemistry which developed between coaches and players, players and players, and these extraordinary individuals who came from disparate backgrounds and environments and who happened to be on the scene together at the right time.

Included in the group of about twenty guys who actually played in the games were farm kids from tiny Iowa towns, big city guys from Chicago, two guys who had been orphaned most of their lives, three guys who had no fathers, older guys who had been in the armed forces for several years or who had bummed around the country during those depression days, younger guys who were just overwhelmed to even be a part of a great university, guys who were bright academically and some who weren't. Only one regular, Ray Murphy, came from a family sufficiently affluent to have sent him to the university without any financial or scholarship assistance, and Murph was one of the toughest, most respected and best liked guys on the squad; the rest of us all came from financially struggling family situations. As a relatively immature youngster, I just couldn't go beyond the surface of the overwhelming things which were happening to us footballers in 1939-1940. After many years I can now look back with some perspective and understanding. I find myself much closer and more appreciative of the coaches, of my teammates and of the people who were part of our "miracle year."

Our football team had a remarkable academic record. Out of forty men still around when the season ended, only one failed to graduate from Iowa. Of the first twenty or so men who actually played the games, every one graduated; there were two retired military colonels, two lawyers and one of them a superior court judge, the others all successful in their post-football, post-college lives. As Erwin Prasse says, "What a great bunch of guys."

Guess I'll wrap it up on that.

Sincerely,

Al Couppee

## 20 September 1985

Dear Scott,

Excuse the long hand as my secretary (wife) is in Cleveland tending to her sick sister. First, I'd like to mention that I had the privilege to play with the greatest group of men that could possibly come together to form a football team. I would also like to say that I had the privilege of playing under two of the greatest coaches in the world. I played under Iowa's Coach of the Year Dr. Eddie Anderson and, in 1943, under the greatest Minnesota coach and former Coach of the Year, Bernie Bierman [when] I was a Naval Aviation Cadet at the Iowa Naval Pre-Flight school.

I personally believe Anderson's philosophy of positive thinking had a great effect upon the team as well as upon individuals, as result of his coaching and teaching I developed greater confidence and determination in attacking the challenges of life. I believe the success of so many members of that squad was due in part to the philosophy of Dr. Anderson.

I had a good game against Northwestern in 1939 which was my first "Big Ten" game as a sophomore. I was the third and last of the centers and they (Northwestern) tried to get me out of the game. I did get banged up quite badly, but I was accustomed to playing the full game in high school with a few hurts. Northwestern had an excellent team—outstanding guards, center and halfback. Hahnenstein, Method, Hayman, DeCorrevant.

We were hurt most when Kinnick injured his shoulder on a defensive play and wasn't able to use his passing arm and was forced to leave the game. I realize that I did at least a satisfactory job, but the important thing was that the coach could have called upon several of the other reserves and they could have done equally as well in their position. I think this indicates the whole squad was equally trained and conditioned to go all the way according to Dr. Eddie's philosophy, "The team that's in the best condition will win." He's the only physician I've known who believed running was the cure for everything from a sprained ankle to a missed signal. As I look at it now I was lucky and pleased to be able to fill the gap created by injuries.

I appreciate your interest and all the work you have done in our behalf.

Sincerely,

George "Red" Frye

## 8 April 1986

Dear Scott,

    I hope you will accept my long overdue apology for not having written you long ago.

    You might be interested in one of my fondest memories of the 1939 season. It involved our opening game against the University of South Dakota, as my brother, Howard, a guard on their team, and I played across the line from each other. Another big thrill for our team was being introduced to Don Ameche, a popular movie star those days, after the Northwestern game. He and Dr. Eddie were close friends. I have so many wonderful memories of that great season—my association with Nile Kinnick among them needless to say. Most of all, however, is the extraordinary bond of friendship which was formed that year and has continued these nearly 47 years. We held our first reunion in 1964, to celebrate our 25th year since the 1939 season, and have continued to meet in Iowa City every five years since then. Far too many have passed away, but those of us still around are looking forward to our 50th reunion in 1989. Dr. Ambrose Callahan, one of our teammates who lived in Sioux City, Iowa, died just last week.

    My wife, Mildred, was a student at Iowa in 1939. I met her that year, incidently, and we have been married since 1943. With every best wish for happiness and success, I remain,

Sincerely yours,

Charles W. Tollefson

## 9 September 1985

Dear Scott,

I was a member of the 1939 squad for about four weeks. I had a knee operation in February of 1939 which was re-injured in October resulting in my having to leave the team.

I remember practices as being intense and well run. In those days we had the three coaches, (1) head coach, (2) line coach, and (3) backfield coach. All coached both offense and defense. I recall a few grad-assistant coaches also helped out.

I received a sound background in coaching techniques and made it my career vocation. I coached nine years in high school and 18 in college. After winning the Wisconsin State High School Basketball Championship in 1949, I invited Dr. Eddie Anderson to be our banquet speaker. It was the highlight of the year when he accepted and spoke. Dr. Eddie was very well received.

Sincerely yours,

Carl Vergamini, Professor Emeritus
University of Wisconsin, Superior

## *1939 Opponents:*

## 17 March 1986

Dear Scott,

I wish I could help you more, but I'll recall what I can about the 1939 Ironmen. First, it was a team without great talent. Rather its strength was unity, hustle, and perfection. In our game, Harmon had a great day and we won 27-7. However, at the end of the game, the Hawks were hitting harder and executing better. It was a team that rallied around Kinnick.

When I say the Ironmen lacked tall and big players, what it really lacked was depth. Couppee, Prasse, Murphy, Enich et al were good players, but when one was injured we ran at his replacement. Consequently, we were able to outman the Hawks and were able to beat them with freshness—the Michigan game was the third that they had to go all the way.

Hope this is some help. Please give my regards to your dad.

Sincerely,

Evy
(Forest Evashevski—Michigan)

## 10 October 1986

Dear Scott,

I certainly remember your father and uncle. They did excellent work, much to my misfortune. As you recall, my teams did not fare too well against the Davenport schools.

The 1939 Iowa game was the only time I played near home during my career. I wanted desperately to do well in that game. Unfortunately I made a mistake at Michigan the preceding week straining my internal lateral ligaments in my left knee. I really wanted to play and said that I was better than I was. Later when I coached I would never ask a player if he was OK. I just would not play him.

Iowa had six excellent players, Dick Evans and Erwin Prasse at ends, Mike Enich, a tackle who I thought was the best player on the Iowa team, Bill Green, a very fast halfback, Al Couppee, a big blocking back, and Nile Kinnick. Kinnick was a very good back doing all things well, but I did not put him in the class with Harmon or Smith. His greatest was inspiring the team to just a little bit more. I doubt if he ever lost, except when time ran out on him. John O'Donnell wanted to have our picture together for the *Democrat* on the following morning's paper. It was done and afterward I said, "Good luck, Nile," and he never answered me with anything.

As for the game, Minnesota played well for three quarters leading Iowa 9-0. Then our line seemed to run out of gas. Why they were not changed, I do not know. We intercepted Kinnick five times, which should be enough to stop any team. As for me, I did not play well. I tried to punt the ball and downed my own punt, after the roll, as it went eleven yards. I did get an interception I believe I fumbled and lost the ball at an inopportune time. I think I remember dropping a third down pass that hit me in the palm of my hands.

My touchdown was a controversial one. All Iowa grandstand quarterbacks are positive that I did not make it. It was a fourth down play, a reverse which Marty Christensen gave me the ball. Van Every made a block on the end which allowed me to get outside, but the halfback forced me to the sideline and drove into him. The ball was in the wrong arm, so when I hit the goal line it was barely over the line. There was an official in the end zone standing on the sideline, and I gave him the ball. Then the referee was following the play having a good look to see if I was out of bounds. I did one thing right that day.

I do not remember the first [Iowa] touchdown, but the second to Bill Green was a well designed play, and our guys gave Nile too much time to throw. I recall that Prasse and Evans ran a crossing pattern in front of me, as I tried to decide which one to cover I looked for the ball and it was in the air going to Green. They really had three men open in the end zone.

They should be given credit for not giving up, and continuing to come after us until the game ended. This is what Kinnick did for that team. For Iowa it was an exciting victory.

Sincerely,

George "Sonny" Franck (Minnesota)

## 15 October 1985

Dear Scott,

    How well I remember the Iowa-Indiana game of 1939. It was so hot that I lost about 20 pounds, and didn't recover until Monday of the following week.

    Iowa had the ball on our 20-yard line and could of kicked a field goal to tie us. I heard Kinnick give some guy hell and said he was calling the play. Well, it was a pass to Prasse that won the game for them.

    It seemed like every time we went ahead of Iowa and thought it was won they would come back. I remember that game because of the heat.

As ever,

Emil "Moose" Uremovich (Indiana)

## 8 July 1986

Dear Scott,

I ran across your letter just the other day, and am sorry that I misplaced it and had not answered before now. One reason could have been that you don't like to think about the unpleasant anymore than you have to . . . you know the final score was 13-9 in that ballgame and it was tough loss for us.

It was a very tough-nosed, hard-fought game right to the end. We did have a 9-7 (or maybe it was 9-6) lead going into that last two minutes. Also, it was interesting to note that I had intercepted a pass with about two minutes to go. Had we been given the ball we could have lasted out the two minutes and been the victor. However, there was an interference penalty called on one of our backs (I think it was Joe Mernick). Evidently one of the ends, that could have been Erwin Prasse, tripped as he jumped over Mernick who had fallen down. Interference was called and that gave Iowa back the ball and in the following plays there was a long pass in the end zone for the touchdown and Iowa came out the victor 13-9.

I remember Al Couppee and others, including Nile Kinnick, and we did have a very fond memory of playing on a pretty great team . . . regardless of the outcome of this particular game.

The best to you. With kindest regards, I am

Sincerely yours,

Harold Van Every, CLU (Minnesota)

## *Other Notables:*

## 19 October 1984

Dear Scott,

Your letter of September 20 brought back a flood of memories. You can hardly do better in coming to know Nile Kinnick as a student, athlete and close associate than through Judge Stuart and Max Hawkins.

I can hardly believe it! I found the original letter I wrote to Nile Kinnick shortly after Pearl Harbor and *Nile's response*. I'm enclosing copies for you. I was a graduate student at Iowa at that time, and editor of *The Daily Iowan*, and he was then in training as a prospective pilot in the Navy, having left the Iowa law school to enlist.

Sincerely,

Loren Hickerson (Friend of Nile Kinnick)

### Saturday December 13, 1941

Dear Loren:

You letter of December 10th addressed to my home in Omaha was forwarded to me here just a day or two ago. This is the second time you have written to me at some length concerning matters of no little importance. The other letter to which I am referring is the one you wrote me shortly after I had received the Heisman Trophy in New York City. Your correspondence in both instances embodied qualities of foresight, inspiration, and fundamental thinking that would command the respect of all serious minded young men. I can assure you, Loren, that each time you struck a responsive chord in my own nature. I feel flattered that you have taken the time to write me in this vein. However, this time, as before, I find myself so busy with unavoidable duties that I shall not be able to reply in a manner that I would like to. I trust that you will understand my situation, and not think me unappreciative of your time, effort, and thought. I, too, heard President Roosevelt deliver his request for a declaration of war against Japan, and I, too, felt that from now on we would be a nation united. You would have been proud of the impatience with which the young men in training down here waited for Congress to vote the might of the United States into action against tyranny. It makes me happy to hear that the student body of Iowa University has finally snapped out of it. It will be a long and bitter road to victory, but victory there will be, and with it the U.S. will have gained the world prestige she long ago should have earned.

I share with you an innate desire to be of public service to my country. It is the lot of our generation to serve as military men first, and then, with an idealism undaunted to enlist with as much zeal to form a lasting peace. All will come right; our cause is just and righteous, this country will not lose. "Let us have faith that right makes might, and in that faith let us to the end dare to do our duty as we understand it."

Yes, Loren, some day I would like to meet you as a fellow Senator or Representative in Washington, D.C. Whether that will ever be my lot none can now say. But for those who have the rightful desire, and expectation, a way is usually opened. Let us hope that you and I, and many, many others like us, will be enabled some day, somewhere, somehow to contribute in some small way to the peace and progress of this world. There is nothing wrong with dreams povided foundations are put under them.

Nice to hear from you again, Loren. Give my best to all who can receive it as a friend. Thumbs up!

Yours,
Nile Kinnick

## 25 September 1988

Dear Scott,

As the fall of 1989 comes around there is certain to be many recollections of the 1939 football season at Iowa University. I hope I will be around to watch and hear. I had my 95$^{th}$ birthday last April, and still feel very much interested. I do not expect to go down [to Iowa City] even if I am still on deck. But I will be listening.

The Documents Library at the University has quite a store of items, such as Nile's diaries during the period of his military service, files of correspondence with his family, family scrap books and many photographs. I sent all of that material to the library several years ago so it might be available after I am gone. Unfortunately there is no exchange of letters with his mother. She carefully destroyed all of his letters to her after his fatal crash in the Gulf of Paria, and she passed in 1966. I am glad you got to browse through the Kinnick material in Bob McCown's custody at Iowa City. As time goes by it is astonishing that Nile's memory still is vivid and undiminished. You have chosen wisely in searching for details of his thinking and actions as I also believe he was a worthy model.

Before answering your questions let me say that I have consistently avoided projecting myself into Nile's story. It is his story and a good one. I love to read what others have to say. It pleases me very much that you want to include the men of the Ironmen team. There is plenty of glory for all of them and every man on the squad played a part in that year's success.

Nile was not closer to any one on the squad than to all of them. It was truly a team effort, all for one and one for all. Nile had an immense appreciation of the coaches, especially Anderson and Carideo. That began with the first appearance of the coaches early in the Spring of 1939. Nile never seriously considered playing professionally in any sport.

I have never seen any description of the play in which Nile's shoulder injury occurred. It was in about the last minute of the third quarter [of the Northwestern game], and he was pulled out when it looked like he was hurt. His mother and I were in the stands but did not see how he was injured. He rode home with us when we drove back to Omaha. His recovery was quick and without complication. The trip to New York for the Heisman was just two weeks later and he appeared normal then. And he played again in the college team against the Green Bay Packers the following August, which I also saw.

The only member of the '39 squad I have met is Ken Pettit. He was from Logan [Iowa] and had enlisted in the Navy Air and was called at the same time as Nile. So he came down from Logan and stayed all night with us the day before they drove to Kansas City to begin training at Fairfax Base on the Kansas side of the river. I can't remember meeting any other player or coach. Ken later lived at Manchester, Iowa, where he was a lawyer and where he died a few years ago. Right after Pearl Harbor a new and much larger air base was started by the Navy, at Olathe, Kansas, about 25 miles SW of Kansas City. In August 1943 the new training hall on that base was being completed and it was dedicated to Nile in a ceremony which I witnessed. Several years later, about 1970, that base was abandoned as a training place.

I saw Bob Feller last in Adel last July when we both were there for a rededication of the Kinnick-Feller Park where Bob and Nile played on the Junior Legion team that centered there. Bob played third base and pitched when a relief was needed. They were about 11 and 12 then and had two years on that team. Nile was the catcher. Just inside the park gate is a splendid monument dedicated to these lads who later gained the highest honors in their respective sports. The first dedication of the park was about 1962 and Bob couldn't be there. Hence the rededication program. Bob's mother, Lena Forret, was in the same high school class with Nile's mother and me in Adel.

I do want to repeat a comment I made to you earlier, that I want you to leave me out of your story as much as possible. There should be no confusion about who you are writing about. Thanks very much.

Kind regards,

Nile Kinnick, Sr.

[Note: The senior Mr. Kinnick passed away in July of 1989, shortly before the 50th anniversary of the Ironmen's football season. He was preceded in death by his three sons, Nile and Ben during World War II—both as pilots—son George in 1987, and the boys' mother, Frances in 1966.]

# CHAPTER 15

## AN INTERVIEW WITH NILE KINNICK

This is the transcript of a radio interview conducted by sports columnist and radio announcer Arch Ward with Nile Kinnick two days before the College All-Star Football Game in Chicago vs. the Green Bay Packers—August 29th, 1940

**Announcer:** First of all, Nile, I wonder if you didn't get a tremendous thrill when you saw that you led the poll for this All-Star game and that you were elected to a starting position at left half-back.

**Nile Kinnick:** Certainly you are right, Arch. Every athlete naturally looks forward to playing in this game and I can tell you that I'm mighty happy to find the support I've gotten from fans all over the country.

**Announcer:** You've got more votes out in Iowa now than Mr. Roosevelt or Mr. Wilke will get in November—it was over a million I believe.

**Nile Kinnick:** Well, certainly solidarity was fine out there in Iowa.

**Announcer:** How do you like it in Evanston? Is everything moving along smoothly?

**Nile Kinnick:** Well, certainly there's a fine bunch of boys congregated out there at Evanston and we're all having a fine time, yet, at the same time we're working mighty hard in preparation for this ball game.

**Announcer:** Do you think you're working as hard as you would at this stage of the season at Iowa?

**Nile Kinnick:** I think we are conducting things on a very similar basis. I don't think the coaches have deviated very much from training regulations or from the workouts on the field or from some of the plays being given.

**Announcer:** So what do you think of the staff of coaches which the fans of the nation elected for this game?

**Nile Kinnick:** I think they've shown very fine judgement. All the coaches are very excellent.

**Announcer:** Well, I think you can talk authoritatively about the head coach at any rate, Dr. [Eddie] Anderson of Iowa. Are you under any special instructor's camp or have you been receiving orders from more than one member of the staff?

**Nile Kinnick:** I think we all have been receiving instruction from nearly all the men on the staff though, frankly, I think I receive the main portion of my instruction from Anderson as I did out at Iowa.

**Announcer:** Well, that would be natural. So, how has Eddie Anderson divided the squad? Has he, for instance, put the half-backs together yet? Or the tackles and centers?

**Nile Kinnick:** He's divided the squad up tentatively into different teams and tried to put the boys who are familiar with his system—his shifts—tried to intersperse them onto different squads in order to help the other boys catch on and so forth.

**Announcer:** Are you lined up with any special unit? If so, who are they?

**Nile Kinnick:** I don't know how long this is going to last, but today and yesterday I was lined up with Banks McFadden and a boy by the name of Jack Knick and Ben Kisch from Pittsburgh.

**Announcer:** In your mind, who have been the outstanding players at Evanston so far?

**Nile Kinnick:** We really haven't done enough yet to say who has stood out, but McFadden looks awful good to me as far as the backs are concerned . . . there is just a host of good boys out there as a matter of fact.

**Announcer:** How do you fellas occupy your spare time?

**Nile Kinnick:** As far as I'm personally concerned, I go to shows or go down along the lake front. I'll go out with the boys and get a Coke in the evening. We take it pretty easy in the evening so we can get out there the next day with a little more vim and vigor

**Announcer:** Are you sorry, Nile, that you're through with your collegiate career at Iowa?

**Nile Kinnick:** I think I face that with mingled emotions. Nearly every football player hates to see it all over, yet at the same time if he finished up in good style he usually has no regrets and is fairly glad that it is over.

**Announcer:** Well, I think that's a sensible outlook. Have you made up your mind what you intend to do?

**Nile Kinnick:** I think that I have made up my mind. I plan to go back to law school in the fall. I really have my heart set on that.

**Announcer:** Where is your home?

**Nile Kinnick:** I live in Omaha, Nebraska right now. I lived in Iowa for a great number of years, but have been in Omaha for the past six.

**Announcer:** Are you one of those fellas up at Evanston who looks every morning for a letter in feminine handwriting before you can really get out there and work?

**Nile Kinnick:** Frankly, I'm not. I wish that I could include myself on that list.

**Announcer:** Maybe we'll see what we can do for you while you're here.

**Nile Kinnick:** [Laughing] Well, that'll be fine.

**Announcer:** Tell us, Nile, what would you consider the greatest thrill you've had in football? And I don't mean having the honor of being selected to a starting position on the All-Star squad.

**Nile Kinnick:** Well, I think that would stand first. But the next thing in line very definitely, as far as I'm concerned, was the win over Minnesota . . . Minnesota is our arch rival out there and beating them gave me the greatest thrill I've ever had in college football.

**Announcer:** I think that would hold for almost anybody. It gave me a great thrill and I was over in Columbus, Ohio that day and when the score came through that Iowa had knocked off Minnesota I just . . . forgot all about my immediate assignment. By the way, Nile, who are some of the All-Star mates that you have up in Evanston that you've played with or against in college football?

**Nile Kinnick:** There are two other boys from Iowa up there at the present time. Buzz Dean, a half-back and Dick Evans, an end. Also, Erwin Prasse was elected, but he's playing baseball at the present time and couldn't get away. There are a great many boys that I played against. Right off the bat I think of Jim Logan from Indiana, he's in the starting line-up. There are boys from Purdue . . . from Minnesota . . . boys from Notre Dame that I can call to mind . . . just a great many boys down there.

**Announcer:** Well, I suppose you fellas from the Western [Big Ten] Conference naturally have more associates up at Northwestern than the boys from the more remote parts of the country. I think we had something like forty from the Midwest on this year's All-Star squad.

**Nile Kinnick:** Well, I think that's only natural.

**Announcer:** Thank you, Nile, for coming up tonight. It was awful nice of you, and I wish you luck on the night of August twenty-ninth in what perhaps will be your farewell [game].

The All-Star Game was played at Chicago's Soldier Field in front of 85,000 fans. Nile Kinnick threw two touchdown passes, and drop-kicked four extra points in a losing effort. The NFL Green Bay Packers defeated the College All-Stars 45-28 in a game that concluded well after midnight. Dr. Eddie Anderson, years later, recalled " . . . I think it was one of the most entertaining games ever played in that series." That fall, Nile Kinnick entered Iowa Law School and helped Anderson coach the football team.

*Nile C. Kinnick, Law School—University of Iowa
(author's collection)*

# BIBLIOGRAPHY—

## PRINT SOURCES

### Books:

Baker, Dr. L. H. *Football Facts and Figures*. Farrar & Rinehart. New York: 1945.

Brady, John T. *The Heisman, A Symbol of Excellence*. Brady Associates. Atheneum, New York: 1984.

Bright, Chuck. *University of Iowa Football—The Hawkeyes*. Strode Publishers. Huntsville, Alabama: 1982.

Cohane, Tim. *Great College Coaches of the Twenties and Thirties*. Arlington House. New York: 1973.

Crisler, H.O. "Fritz". *Modern Football*. McGraw-Hill. New York: 1949.

Danzig, Allison. *The History of American Football: Its Great Teams, Players, and Coaches*. Prentice-Hall. Upper Saddle River, New Jersey: 1956.

Hyman, Mervin D. and Gordon S. White, Jr. *Big Ten Football*. Macmillan. New York: 1977.

Lamb, Dick and Bert McGrane. *75 Years with the Fighting Hawkeyes*. William C. Brown. Dubuque, Iowa: 1964.

McCallum, John D. *Big Ten Football Since 1895*. Chilton Books. Radnor, Pennsylvania: 1976.

McCallum, John D and Charles H. Pearson. *College Football USA—1869-1971*. McGraw-Hill: New York. 1972.

Schoor, Gene. *100 Years of Notre Dame Football.* Avon Books. New York: 1987.

Stump, Derald W. *Kinnick: The Man and the Legend.* University of Iowa Press. Iowa City, Iowa: 1975.

## Periodicals: (Various Articles from each)

*Ann Arbor News.* Ann Arbor, Michigan.
*Cedar Rapids Gazette.* Cedar Rapids, Iowa.
*Chicago Tribune.* Chicago, Illinois.
*Colliers Magazine*
*Daily Iowan.* Iowa City, Iowa.
*Des Moines Register.* Des Moines, Iowa.
*New York Times.*
*Press Citizen.* Iowa City, Iowa.
*Quad City Times.* Davenport, Iowa.
*Saturday Evening Post Magazine.*
*Time Magazine.*